SOUL IN THE STORM

Stress Management Through Mindfulness and Inner Transformation

NANCY WAGAMAN

Copyright © 2020 Nancy Wagaman. All rights reserved.
Published by Applied Conscious Technologies, LLC, in San Diego, CA, USA.

Legal Notice: It is illegal to reproduce, store in a retrieval system, or transmit in any form or by any means, electronic, mechanical, photocopying, recording, or otherwise, this book in whole or in part without the prior written permission of the author. This book is sold subject on the condition that it shall not, by way of trade or otherwise, be lent, resold, hired out, or otherwise circulated without the publisher's prior consent in any form other than that in which it is published and without a similar condition including this condition being imposed on the subsequent purchaser.

Disclaimer Notice: By accessing any content in this book or external content associated with this book (collectively referred to as "this content"), you agree that you are solely responsible for the use of this content and for any risks and results of doing so, and that the author, her companies, and publisher, and other associated entities are under no circumstances responsible or liable in any way for the use of this content or for direct or indirect losses or other undesired situations occurring as a result of the use of this content. You acknowledge that the author and said entities are not rendering medical or professional mental health advice, diagnosis, or treatment, and you agree to seek professional help immediately if you are experiencing mental or physical distress, if you have thoughts of harming yourself or others, if you are unable to control yourself, or if you or someone else is in danger of harm. If you or anyone else are at risk or in imminent danger, you are responsible for ensuring that the dangerous situation is averted or resolved completely. No warranties and no guarantees of any particular result or outcome are expressed or implied.

If you do not agree to be bound by all of these terms, do not access the content of this book or its associated external content.

ISBN: 978-0-9985459-7-4 (print)
ISBN: 978-0-9985459-6-7 (ebook)
Library of Congress Control Number: 2020914899
Printed in the U.S.A.
NancyWagamanBooks.com
10 9 8 7 6 5 4 3 2 1

*To the wise ones who have guided us through the ages
and to the wise heart within each of us.*

Contents

About This Book vii

PART I SOUL AS HAVEN 1
   Chapter 1-1 You Are Soul 3
   Chapter 1-2 Getting to Soul 7

PART II SOUL-CENTERED STRESS MANAGEMENT 13
   Chapter 2-1 Stress and the Soul 15
   Chapter 2-2 Using the Techniques in This Book 27

PART III HAVEN-BUILDING TOOLKIT 35
   About This Toolkit 37
   Chapter 3-1 Working Through an Issue 38
   Chapter 3-2 Acceptance 43
   Chapter 3-3 Responsibility 46
   Chapter 3-4 Processing Emotions 58
   Chapter 3-5 Forgiveness 61
   Chapter 3-6 Reframing 65
   Chapter 3-7 Transforming Beliefs 68
   Chapter 3-8 Setting Intentions 71
   Chapter 3-9 Transforming Negative Self-Talk 75
   Chapter 3-10 Exploring Projections 78
   Chapter 3-11 Revisiting Past Decisions 85
   Chapter 3-12 Completing Unfinished Business 87
   Chapter 3-13 Renegotiating Outdated Agreements 90
   Chapter 3-14 Decision Making 95
   Chapter 3-15 Leaning into Your Strengths 99
   Chapter 3-16 Creating More of What You Want 104
   Chapter 3-17 Deepening Your Spirituality 110
   Chapter 3-18 Spiritual Exercises 114
   Chapter 3-19 Rainbow Visualization 118
   Chapter 3-20 Affirmations 120
   Chapter 3-21 Meditation 124
   Chapter 3-22 Free-Form Writing 127
   Chapter 3-23 Writing a Shred Letter 132
   Chapter 3-24 Mental Clean-Sweep 135
   Chapter 3-25 Sleep 138
   Chapter 3-26 Dream Interpretation 144
   Chapter 3-27 Dealing with Nightmares 153

PART IV QUICK-FIX TOOLKIT 161
   About This Toolkit 163
   Chapter 4-1 Calling in the Light (Quick Version) 164
   Chapter 4-2 Centering 165

Contents

Chapter 4-3 10-Second Stress-Release Valve 167
Chapter 4-4 1-Minute Peace Meditation 168
Chapter 4-5 Prayer 169
Chapter 4-6 Perspective 171
Chapter 4-7 Identifying Your Next Step 173
Chapter 4-8 Preparation and Contingency Planning 174
Chapter 4-9 Releasing Undesired Dynamics 175
Chapter 4-10 Releasing Imagined Scenarios 178
Chapter 4-11 Observing Your Thoughts 181
Chapter 4-12 Setting Aside a Worry 182
Chapter 4-13 Focusing on a Keyword 183
Chapter 4-14 Gratitude 184
Chapter 4-15 Visualization 185
Chapter 4-16 Speaking to Love 187
Chapter 4-17 Seeing Others as Souls 188
Chapter 4-18 Letting Go of Shoulds 189
Chapter 4-19 Thinking Locally 192
Chapter 4-20 Reality Check 194
Chapter 4-21 Using Distraction 196
Chapter 4-22 Inspiration 197
Chapter 4-23 Focused Breathing 199
Chapter 4-24 Heart Touchstones 200
Chapter 4-25 Energy Work 201
Chapter 4-26 Social Discernment 204
Chapter 4-27 Environmental Discernment 206
Chapter 4-28 Physical Contact 208
Chapter 4-29 Water 209
Chapter 4-30 Music 210

PART V QUICK REFERENCE **211**

What Did You Think of This Book? 215
Keep Exploring 217
More Books by Nancy Wagaman 219
About the Author 223
Index 225

About This Book

Anytime you experience stress you have the power to transform it into inner peace, if you have the right tools. As the soul that you are, your natural inner state is peace. Any stressful disturbances within you are merely temporary dynamics obscuring that peace. When you understand how to shift those dynamics, neutralize stress reactions, and move into the peace of soul in any moment, you discover true freedom within.

A Practical Approach to Stress
In this book you'll learn a practical approach to stress management using mindfulness and soul-centered inner transformation. The personal-growth focus of this book draws from various modern disciplines, ancient enlightenment philosophy, decades of professional work, and personal soul-searching (and soul-finding). The 57 easy-to-follow techniques included here were chosen for their effectiveness and upliftment in a wide range of situations. As you read (as in all of life), I encourage you to use what works for you and let go of the rest. Whatever you do use, apply it in a way that benefits and uplifts you.

Soul as a Theory
Soul is theoretical. It may or not exist, at least from a scientific perspective (at least using the scientific methods of measurement developed thus far). However, *something* exists that we call "soul." This book focuses on that *something* we'll call "soul"—based primarily on my firsthand experiences (since it would be impossible for me to give a firsthand account of someone else's inner world). Regardless of your beliefs about soul or whether you've experienced it personally, you can use the *idea of soul* to your benefit as a model to create a more peaceful situation within yourself.

Terminology
Words are simply labels used to describe things we want to talk about. Some of the concepts in this book are nebulous, vague, or challenging to describe precisely in words. Many of the concepts are ones that we humans

don't understand fully or talk about often, or that may even be completely new and unfamiliar to you. As you read, I suggest connecting with the concepts themselves rather than getting hung up on the words used to describe them. For example, "Soul" may not be the real or best name for soul. I call it "soul" here, but you can call it anything that resonates with you: essence, Divine self, the "I" of "I am," "the higher me," or something else. Likewise, I use "the Divine" to refer to the highest power—which you might choose to think of as God, holiest of holies, creator, source of pure love, or some other name. As you read, you can substitute names with which you feel comfortable, according to your personal preference.

Scope

This book focuses on a practical, soul-centered approach to managing psychological stress. For more about the consciousness as a whole (including physical, mental, emotional, soul, intuition, etc.), refer to "A Model of Consciousness" in other books I've written, including *The Curious Dreamer's Practical Guide to Dream Interpretation.*

This is not a religious book. In it, I refer to soul as it truly exists: independent of religion or any other human-devised construct, as souls have existed for eons before those constructs were created.

Taking Responsibility for You

In reading this book, it's up to you to use the information here only in ways that benefit you for greater well-being. That may mean choosing to not use certain parts if they don't work well for you. If at any time you feel overwhelmed beyond your control or if you need help, seek professional assistance. This book isn't to be used in place of therapy or other professional treatment. (For the terms to which you indicate agreement by reading this book, see the Copyright page.)

PART I

SOUL AS HAVEN

Chapter 1-1

You Are Soul

In This Chapter:
Peace is Present 3
Soul as Respite 4
Envisioning Soul 4
Experiencing Soul 5

We each have within us a light that is more powerful than any stress or emotion. Within this light no darkness can exist. When the winds of stress and anxiety whip around you, turn to this light within and you'll find a haven of such profound peace that the storm cannot touch you. Though it may rage, the storm cannot intrude into the haven of soul.

Peace is Present

Peace already exists within you. There's a reason that the saying is "finding peace" instead of "creating peace" or "thinking about peace." At all times there is already a place of peace within you, and you merely need to touch into it. It may be buried underneath layers of stress, emotion, mental chatter, imaginings, or whatever else is going on in your consciousness—but it's there. You can move into that peace whenever you choose by shifting your focus there.

To illustrate this, think of a time in your past when you experienced great peace. Maybe a childhood situation or environment in which you felt safe and loved, a person whose presence in your life always calmed you, an experience of nature's glorious beauty, or something else that awakened your inner light or seemed to make everything okay. You may notice that just by thinking of that situation you're starting to feel more peaceful. What's happening is you're revisiting the same peace within your yourself that you experienced back then. That place of peace didn't reside out in the environment or in the person you were with at the time. It was within you—and it still is.

Soul as Respite

Beyond the physical and mental levels within which you conduct your daily life is a whole realm of profound peace within you: soul. Soul exists at a level where none of the disturbances of the lower level can reach, which means stress, hurt, and upset can't breach its perfect peace.

Because you *are* a soul, soul is always present within you. It is the most essential you, the purest form of you. You are a soul who is experiencing life as a human. The rest of you—your lower levels which include body, mind, and emotions—are merely the means through which you (as a soul) experience the earthly world. When you're focused on a swirling storm of everyday stresses in those lower levels, you may not be aware of your "soulness." However, at any time you can elevate your awareness toward the soul level to experience its peace. This book will show you how.

Envisioning Soul

If a human being were a tree, its soul would be its roots: they're an integral part of the tree, but they reach deep into its vital, life-giving source of nourishment. Also, the more strongly established the root system, the more resilient the tree in the face of crisis. The roots hold the tree firm amidst external stresses, and they also provide the sustenance necessary for repair and recovery from those stresses. They are the key to the tree's survival and it could not live without them. Likewise, soul keeps us rooted into the vital sustenance of our lifeforce and holds us steady through physical, mental, and emotional challenges.

However, there's one aspect of this tree model that doesn't quite fit. We tend to think of soul as the "higher" part of a person (higher as in "rising above" or "raising your consciousness"), rather than a "lower" part like a tree's roots. In reality, the soul isn't physically "higher" or "lower" than anything else, although it makes sense to think of it as the "highest" aspect of self. So in this model maybe we can envision the tree as growing upside down, hanging in midair with its roots (soul) facing skyward and integrated with its vital, "higher source" (a "higher power"). Then envision the branches and leaves (your body, emotions, mind, etc.) facing downward into the earthly world (the "lower" physical, mental, and emotional levels). Both parts are living and functioning, but in different realms (sky representing higher awareness and earth representing worldly awareness). If you want to see what's going on in the (physical, mental, emotional) tree canopy, you go look there. But if you want to become aware of the roots (soul), you must "rise above" or "elevate" your consciousness to shift there. You'll learn more about how to do that in "Getting to Soul" (p. 7).

Experiencing Soul

It's challenging to find words to describe the experience of the soul level because it's beyond our usual day-to-day experiences. Some have described it as bliss, peace, joy, a sea of love, perfect well-being, and divine. It could also be described as a deep knowing that everything is okay, or a sense of "home" that feels safe and secure.

Whatever words we use to label it, one thing is for sure: when you're experiencing soul, you know it. You'll feel immediately different when you shift toward soul. Because the stresses and worries of the day can't reach into soul, they will fade away as you elevate your consciousness in the direction of soul. Instead, you'll begin to experience a magnificent sense of peace—a sense of "glowing" from within.

The following sections provide more detail to help you recognize soul when you experience it.

Soul Is Peace

Soul brings a deep experience of peace that's so profound it's indescribable. At the same time, there aren't any "non-peace" elements on the soul level: no stress, anger, fear, judgment, envy, insecurity, lack, etc. because they can't extend above the lower levels. Shifting your awareness toward soul elevates you beyond those, although they may still be there when you return your focus to the lower levels. (There are also ways to eliminate those lower-level negative dynamics, which we'll get to in "The Steps for Getting to Soul," p. 7, and in greater detail in "Part III: Haven-Building Toolkit," p. 35.)

Soul Is Love

Soul expresses only unconditional love and goodwill. It loves with no requirements or restrictions, asking nothing in return. It is actively loving all the time, always benevolent. Soul loves you, others, the world, everything—because love is the soul's true nature.

Soul Is Light

Soul is filled with light. Its light is so intense and complete that there can be no darkness: no hurt, hate, anger, or suffering. If you've ever heard the term "dark night of the soul," it's more about the shadow created within a person when they have turned away from or are blocking out the light of soul within themselves than it is about actual darkness in the soul. The soul's light always shines, and it's up to you whether and when you look toward it. Whenever you choose, you can use the soul's light as a tool for peace, healing, and transformation on the lower levels by calling the light to those areas (see "Calling in the Light," p. 17).

Soul Accepts

Soul accepts everything and everyone. The soul doesn't judge itself (you) or try to tell you what to do. No matter what's happening on your emotional and mental levels, the soul is always accepting and benevolent. The soul can't be "darkened" by any of those negative, lower-level dynamics because they can't reach that high. The soul doesn't find fault with others or hold grudges, but instead accepts that everyone and everything *is as it is in every moment*. It doesn't try to change things (perhaps because it realizes that in the big picture everything is okay). Death, loss, grief, hurt, and anger are all accepted, as the soul extends only loving into all situations.

Soul Is Strong

Soul can't be harmed, broken, or destroyed. It's untouchable by anything in the lower levels (physical, mental, emotional, etc.), which means it can't be wounded by hurt or limited by doubt. It doesn't get tired and it never gives up. No soul can become lost or a "lost cause." The soul doesn't fear death, perhaps because it can't die. The soul is fearless. You might say that soul is the closest thing to a superpower that a human has. Soul is our power of invincibility.

Soul Is Perfect

Soul is perfect as it is. It is complete. It wants for nothing and needs nothing: not love, admiration, or praise. Money means nothing to it. It doesn't crave freedom because it's already free. It doesn't seek to fulfill itself in any way because it is already whole. The soul perceives all through its perfect acceptance and loving. It doesn't wish people were better or the world a nicer place. Seen through the eyes of soul, the world and everyone in it are gloriously beautiful. The soul is in love with all it sees because the soul *exists* in love. So immaculately, gorgeously, perfect is the soul that you might call it "divinely perfect."

Chapter 1-2
Getting to Soul

In This Chapter:
The Steps for Getting to Soul 7
1. Center in Soul 8
2. Remove Obstructions to Soul 9
3. Deepen into Soul 10
Committing to Soul 11

First of all, "Getting to Soul" is a bit of a misnomer. If you actually *are* a soul, how can you "get to" soul? Let me explain, as least the way I experience it: soul is a person's essence, the most authentic self. It's always there, but it gets obscured by the lower-level activity in the consciousness such as thoughts, emotions, imaginings, judgments, inner dialogue, senses, and so on. Focusing on those dynamics actually anchors us in the lower levels of consciousness, which are useful and productive for living in the physical world. However, we need to elevate beyond them to fully experience soul and the peace it provides. So when I talk about "getting to soul," I'm referring to learning to shift your awareness beyond whatever obstructs your experience of soul—beyond the "not peace" dynamics of your consciousness—and focus into the higher level of soul.

Because soul exists in a place where imagination, emotions, and mind can't reach, they can't take you to soul. You won't find soul by imagining it, thinking about it, or trying to feel it emotionally. The only way to experience soul is by elevating your awareness beyond those lower levels.

The Steps for Getting to Soul

The practical steps for "getting to soul" are:
1. Center in Soul.
2. Remove Obstructions to Soul.
3. Deepen into Soul.

You can take these steps in any order, and ideally you'll be using all of them often, because the ongoing practice is the key. Life often demands that we focus in the lower levels (such as while mentally doing taxes or emotionally expressing sadness). But when that's done we can shift awareness back to soul.

Each step helps make the others easier. For example, "Step 1: Center in Soul" immediately shifts your consciousness above and beyond the obstructions in "Step 2: Remove Obstructions to Soul." The obstructions still exist and you can take steps to remove them permanently later (see "Part III: Haven-Building Toolkit," p. 35), but for the moment your consciousness is focused on a level beyond them. Likewise, "Step 3: Deepen into Soul" strengthens your focus into soul awareness, and each time you practice moving there the shift becomes easier and more familiar. And the more time you spend in that elevated state, the more your roots grow there and your experience deepens.

Now let's take a more in-depth look at each of the three steps.

1. Center in Soul

Shift your awareness into the soul that you are. Focusing into soul can immediately bring greater clarity, peace, and healing. The idea is very basic: you shift your awareness to soul by *intending* to do so. Your consciousness will learn to make the transition more easily as you practice more. When you're starting out, you may find it helpful to prepare for the shift this way:

- Connect with your most essential self by acknowledging that you are soul, beyond everything thing else that makes up who you are.
- Affirm that on the most essential level you are soul, and it's your true nature to be peace and to be love.

Here are a few methods that can help prompt this shift instantly (and you can find many more in "Part III: Haven-Building Toolkit," p. 35, and "Part IV: Quick-Fix Toolkit," p. 161):

Keywords

You can use a centering keyword or phrase by saying it inwardly, with the intention to shift your awareness into soul. Examples include:

- "I am soul."
- "I am love."
- "I am Divine soul."

Centering Statements

You could also use a longer statement to center in soul, such as:

- "I am centering myself in soul, drawing deeply from the well of my Divine essence."
- "I call myself forward into the peace of soul."

For more ideas, see "Chapter 4-2: Centering" (p. 165).

Heart Touchstones

Thinking of someone you love unconditionally (parent, child, pet, etc.) can elevate your consciousness into soul. You'll feel your energy shift—a sensation of filling with heartfelt love and simultaneously a releasing of physical, mental, and emotional tensions. (For more details, see "Chapter 4-24: Heart Touchstones," p. 200.)

Focus on Gratitude

Gratitude can instantly elevate your consciousness, especially if it's particularly genuine and heartfelt. When you focus on a person or situation for which you're truly grateful, you'll notice a change within you as your center of focus shifts toward soul. Examples include:

- "I'm grateful for my child, who teaches me unconditional love."
- "I'm grateful for the great friends I have around me."
- "I'm grateful for the joy I receive by helping others in need."

For more about the practice and benefits of gratitude, see "Chapter 4-14: Gratitude" (p. 184).

2. Remove Obstructions to Soul

Remove what obstructs your experience of soul so you can experience soul more directly in your daily life. This step involves clearing away the lower-level dynamics within your consciousness that interfere with experiencing the soul that you are. In other words, you're removing the things that are "not peace" in order to experience the peace that already exists within soul.

You accomplish this by working through inner issues—a process that involves releasing, dissolving, shifting, or resolving each issue's underlying dynamics (judgments, self-defeating beliefs, negative self-talk, outdated decisions, etc.). Until you work through your issues, they continue to not only disturb and distract you, but they're also constantly drawing your focus down into the lower (mental and emotional) levels and away from soul awareness.

Part I: Soul as Haven

What's really beautiful is that the process of working through your issues not only helps clear the way to experience the peace of soul, it's also what's needed to heal and bring light into the areas of your consciousness that are in "darkness" or in need of healing.

This step is not actually a single step but an ongoing process. The idea is to work through whatever issue arises in any given moment. You couldn't work through all your issues at once even if you wanted to, because most issues require individual processes. So you just address whatever is present within you at a given time.

Upcoming parts of this book will delve into much more detail on how to remove these obstructions to soul, beginning with the preliminaries in "Part II: Soul-Centered Stress Management" (p. 13) and then the practical techniques in "Part III: Haven-Building Toolkit" (p. 35).

3. Deepen into Soul

Deepen the roots of your awareness in soul over time through focus and practice.
In this step you pick up where you left off in Step 1, now extending more deeply into soul. This step involves an ongoing process in which you're building your stronghold within soul by spending more time in a state of soul awareness. You can do this by regularly practicing techniques that elevate your awareness into soul (see more at the end of this section), supporting your process with an intention (see "Chapter 3-8: Setting Intentions," p. 71) and a commitment to soul (see "Committing to Soul," p. 11).

You could imagine this deepening process as if you were a tree growing a more extensive root structure. Stronger and deeper roots can better maintain life force, deliver sustenance, and provide a resilient foundation for survival and regeneration.

This deepening process also has a time factor to it: the longer you focus into soul—one second, the next second, the next minute, and so on—the more your experience of soul can benefit you. Also, the more cumulative time you hold your focus there over weeks, months, and years, the more benefit you'll see.

One of the most effective techniques for elevating your consciousness is spiritual exercises, an active inner process during which you shift your awareness beyond the lower levels into soul (see "Chapter 3-18: Spiritual Exercises," p. 114). You can also support this deepening process by practicing unconditional love ("Applying Love," p. 20), setting intentions such as "I intend to shift my awareness into soul" ("Chapter 3-8: Setting Intentions," p. 71), improving and practicing your spirituality ("Chapter 3-17:

Deepening Your Spirituality," p. 110), and any other process that elevates your consciousness (including many others in this book).

Committing to Soul

A soul commitment is a powerful step to establish your awareness of yourself as a soul and to center your focus firmly in soul, ongoing. This involves making an agreement with yourself for your entire being to be in accord with soul ongoing. The word "accord" is based on a Latin root that means something like "to be heart to heart with" or "to be next to the central part." So in making this commitment, you are deciding to live centered in soul, in the "heart" or "most central part" of your being. Through this commitment, you're choosing to live in a soul-centered way, to see yourself and the world through the eyes of soul, and to live from that place of unconditional love and haven of peace within you.

This commitment can take any form you like, but the idea is to choose a form that will have lasting meaning to you and that you'll remember and honor over the long term. A clear intention is more important than the exact words you use. Make this commitment by stating it inwardly, writing it on a piece of paper to keep, or any form that's meaningful to you.

Some examples of a soul commitment statement are:

- "I awaken into my true being as a soul, and I commit to living a soul-centered life."
- "I commit to live in soul accord, centering in the light of soul now and always."
- "I honor the soul that I am. From now on, I commit to living from my soul center, nourished by profound light, love, and peace within."
- "I am soul. I commit to acknowledge and honor myself as a light-filled, loving soul always."

PART II

SOUL-CENTERED STRESS MANAGEMENT

Chapter 2-1
Stress and the Soul

In This Chapter:
Stress Comes from Within 15
Shifting the Locus of Control 17
Calling in the Light 17
Sending the Light 19
Applying Love 20
Mind Mastery 23
Working Your Process 25
Rules of Stress Management 25

When you shift your awareness into soul, you're lifting to a higher level where stress can't reach. Stress may still exist on the lower levels (mental, emotional, etc.), but you don't experience it directly when elevated to a level beyond.

A soul-centered approach to stress involves not only focusing into soul for immediate stress relief, but also the two ongoing processes of deepening into soul and removing inner dynamics that obstruct your experience of soul. And as it turns out, those obstructions *are sources of stress* themselves. More specifically, what you experience as stress is a reaction you've created to something, which then becomes "not peace" within you (and therefore detracts from experiencing soul).

Stress Comes from Within

Stress is a reaction created within yourself rather than something out in the world. Most times when you're experiencing stress, you're actually *stressing yourself* by the way you're reacting to a particular trigger from within your consciousness (a worrisome thought, an imagined scenario, etc.) or from the environment around you (a news report, an angry person, etc.).

An event is only a stress trigger if you react to it in a stressful way. Events themselves are actually neutral: they just "are." You only experience them as stressful when you interpret them as "bad," "wrong," "scary," etc. So it's not the event that's stressful, but rather the way you're *experiencing* or *interpreting* that event.

You can only experience stress within your own consciousness. Your stress can't originate in the outside world because your consciousness is not out there to experience it. Your consciousness is within you. Think about it this way: if a disaster were happening around you but you were asleep and your consciousness wasn't aware of it, you wouldn't feel stressed because you wouldn't be experiencing it or interpreting it in any way. But as soon as you became aware of the trigger you might create a reaction that feels stressful.

The same is true of most forms of stress. When you're feeling overwhelmed, the overwhelm is a reaction you've created within yourself (perhaps you're trying to think about too many things at once or you're allowing your emotions to take charge). In these cases, it might be more accurate to say you're "overwhelming yourself." When you're worried about an upcoming decision, that worry is likely your reaction to the outcomes you're imagining (perhaps because you don't have enough information for the choice to be clear). Perhaps it's more accurate to say you're "worrying yourself."

What's so fortunate is that because stress originates within your consciousness, you can shift it. Because your consciousness is your own domain, you are in charge of what happens there. You are responsible for your own reactions, and being responsible for them means having power over them (we'll discuss this further in "Chapter 3-3: Responsibility," p. 46). For example, in the case of feeling overwhelmed you could stop "overwhelming yourself" by changing the way you perceive and react to the situation, such as by focusing only on identifying your next step (see "Chapter 4-7: Identifying Your Next Step," p. 173), deciding to think about only one thing at a time, or organizing your mental to-do list (see "Chapter 3-24: Mental Clean-Sweep," p. 135). You might stop "worrying yourself" about an upcoming decision by taking the logical approach of considering options and outcomes, and delaying the decision until you have more information (see "Chapter 3-14: Decision Making," p. 95).

(Another form of stress is physical stress, such as due to physical illness or overworking your body. Managing physical stress involves changes like reducing physical activity, managing your schedule, fostering wellness, treating physical ailments, or other approaches as recommended by your physician. For the purposes of this book, we'll focus on nonphysical types of stress.)

Shifting the Locus of Control

Reducing your stress doesn't imply that you deny a problem, ignore an issue, or fail to deal with things you really need to deal with. You can't escape your own responsibility or deny reality (you actually might for a while, but that can lead to even less desirable results in the long run). Rather, truly reducing stress requires the opposite: acceptance and responsibility. These are two of the most transformative, empowering tools in the face of stress because they internalize your locus of control. Choosing to accept that something is the way it is in the moment, and then accepting responsibility for what is yours, puts you directly in charge so you can make decisions and take action. Sometimes that action is external (such as to stop playing a video game or stop eating sweets because of the stressful effect on you) and sometimes it's within your consciousness (such as to stop stressing yourself with inner statements like "everything is horrible" or "I can't do anything right").

Calling in the Light

When you're experiencing stress, "calling in the light" can bring you peace and help shift the situation. Light is the vital lifeforce of the soul. You can think of light as "the essence of life," "Divine light," or the light in the "light vs. dark" theme, such as the benevolent "force" in the *Star Wars* movies. When working with the light, a clear intention is much more important than the name you use to refer to it. When your intention is to work with the light (or whatever you choose to call it), you're working with it itself rather than with the label.

In moments of stress we're also often experiencing frustration, lack of mental clarity, and perhaps enough emotional turmoil that we're not in touch with our intuition and higher wisdom. It wouldn't be surprising when you're stressed if you felt like you didn't know the answers, what's best for you, or even the next step. Even in the clearest state none of us know with certainty what's best in every moment, especially given all the possible consequences and "ripple effects" of a particular action. This sense of "not knowing" can contribute to your stress even more. When you're feeling stressed, unclear, or in doubt, calling in the light can help tremendously.

Calling in the light is like applying an all-purpose balm to all levels of your being. Light can transform darkness, but darkness has no power over light, so the light can illuminate and dissipate darkness within you. This means it can transform mental and emotional disturbances within you, or help you to take action in that direction (see more in "Working Your Process," p. 25). Light can relieve upset, enhance clarity, engender peace, enable healing, or anything else that's for the highest good. Light can also be a catalyst in any process and seems to make things go more smoothly, often with less stress and distress. And when you call in the light "for the highest good of all concerned," these benefits extend to everyone involved in the situation or potentially affected by it in the future. When you call in the light, you may notice great peace and grace in whatever process follows next.

How to Call in the Light
To call in the light, say inwardly or outwardly one of the following:
- "I call in the light and ask for the highest good of all concerned."
- "I ask for the light to fill, surround, and protect me for the highest good of all concerned."
- "I align with the light and with the highest good of all concerned."

You can also just shorten this to "Light for the highest good" or even just "Light" as long as your intention is still the same. It's your intention that directs and enacts this process.

The Highest Good of All Concerned
In case you're thinking that maybe you don't want to wish "good" for someone who has harmed you or whom you don't like, you actually do. That's because when you say, "I call in the light for the highest good of all concerned," those words take into account what that person actually needs in terms of their personal development and becoming the best human being they can be (kinder, wiser, or whatever opportunities are best for their growth and healing), as well as beneficial effects that their actions might have for others, and a whole host of other causes and effects that you could never predict. You don't have to know what that person needs. Since none of us actually *know* what's best for others or what they truly need in their personal development process, "the highest good of all concerned" is a convenient safety mechanism. When you invoke it, you may experience a huge outflowing of your stress, judgments, animosity, efforts to figure out every little detail of what "should" happen to others, and so on.

Light Always

Calling in the light is helpful anytime, not just in times of stress. Whenever you call in the light, you're aligning with love, perfect protection, win-win situations for yourself and others, and the best processes and results for everyone involved—even those of which you're not aware or can't anticipate. I also suggest calling in the light every time you begin an inner process (such as the techniques in this book), regularly throughout the day, and at bedtime.

Sending the Light

When you're dealing with a challenging person or situation, sending the light to that person or situation can bring you peace and can also help shift the situation (similar to calling in the light). Sending the light is along the lines of "sending good thoughts," "sending thoughts and prayers," or "sending good vibrations," but with two major differences. First, the light is the highest, most powerful, purest energy there is (more so than thoughts, prayers, vibrations, or anything else)—and second, the light is sent *through* you, not *from* you.

When you send light, you're not sending it out of your own personal resources. You don't lose anything of yourself when you send it. That's because you're actually directing light from the vast source of it that already exists and that's available to everyone (although some individuals may not be *experiencing* it if they're focused away from it). Your intention to send the light creates a path through which the light can then flow from that source, through you, and then to that person.

You can send light anywhere—to someone else, a group, the world, or anyone and anywhere you choose. You can also send it to yourself, which is basically the same as calling in the light.

Sending the light is of great benefit to both you and whomever you're sending it to, since you get to experience the light as it first moves through you and then to the other person. Light has great power to shift situations involving multiple people toward goodwill, win-win scenarios, harmony in relationships, higher ideals, healing, and peace. The simple act of sending the light can result in astounding transformation within yourself and others.

Keep in mind that once you've sent the light, it's been sent—it is now present with the person or situation to which you sent it. You don't need to keep repeating your request in every moment. However, you can send it anytime you like.

Applying Love

If light is the vital lifeforce of the soul, then love is the language of the soul. Everything the soul expresses is communicated through the language of unconditional love. That's because soul resides on a higher level than the "not love" and "not peace" dynamics of the emotional and mental levels. In the realm of soul, everything is "of love." And because each of us is a soul, we are "of love" (which we experience more and more as the lower-level disturbances are cleared away).

Love has the power to heal. That's a familiar phrase, and it's true. Unconditional love is the healing elixir of the soul. It's more powerful than any thought, emotion, or stressful reaction. It can infuse all areas of consciousness, dissolving negativity and filling every dark corner. Unconditional love offers a cure for emotional wounds and a remedy for judgments and misunderstandings. You have this magnificent force of unconditional love within you to call on anytime, including in times of stress. A primary rule of soul-centered living is: **Always love.**

(If the word "love" doesn't work for you, call it something else: goodwill, positive regard, benevolence, or heartlight. You can label it practically anything you want and it will still be the same thing if your intention is clear.)

How to Apply Unconditional Love

You love unconditionally by choosing to love unconditionally. It's that simple.

Choose to Love

Love is a choice, more than an action you take or something you do. As always within your consciousness, you are in charge. You can choose unconditional love in any moment, and it only takes an instant to shift into that higher level that is loving. If you like, you can use a keyword to help make that shift, such as "I love" or "goodwill."

Love Without Expectation

When you're loving unconditionally, your love needs no reason or expectation of anything in return. It doesn't say, "I love because..." or "I'd love you if only..." or "I'd love you more if...." Unconditional love *loves at maximum power*—everyone, everything, all the time, no matter what.

Unconditional love doesn't place any conditions on the other person. In the moment you choose unconditional love, you set aside all expectations, requirements, exceptions, and other restrictions that would control when your love will or won't be given. You find goodwill within yourself, regardless of anything else going on. You love regardless of your judgments or beliefs, the labels you've put on the situation, the other person's actions or appearance, or anything else that would impede your goodwill for that person or situation. You love even if you don't feel like loving and even if you don't feel like there's any love within yourself to give (which often is the exact time that you most need experience loving within yourself). You simply choose love.

Practicing unconditional love doesn't mean you have to like, agree with, or want to spend time with whomever or whatever you're loving unconditionally. It's possible to experience a person as very unpleasant and still choose to love them unconditionally. It's also possible to not like a particular aspect of yourself but choose to love it unconditionally anyway.

A Higher Love

Keep in mind that unconditional love is not the same as the attachment or desire of romantic love, or the kind of love that attempts to control, influence, or posses another person. You may feel unconditional love for a romantic partner, but that higher love exists beyond any demands or attachment you have to the person or relationship. You can recognize unconditional love because it always has goodwill toward and wants the best for the other person.

Also beware of emotional love—the kind of "love" you feel toward someone when you want to hug them so hard it hurts them or you want them to stay when the best thing for them is to be elsewhere. That kind of love comes from the emotional level rather than the higher soul level, and it can actually be destructive if it's allowed to operate in a way that's disconnected from unconditional love.

Love Comes from Within

Unconditional love exists within you, independent of anyone or anything outside yourself. When you look upon another person through the eyes of soul, that love is originating within yourself rather than with that other person.

"I love you" is an action statement. "I love" describes your choice to love, and "you" describes the direction in which you're choosing to send that love. If it's possible for you to feel that love when the person isn't with you, or even after they've passed away, the love *must* be coming from within you. When you're experiencing unconditional love toward someone, consider that the way it's working is this: Seeing or thinking of that person is prompting you to shift into soul awareness and love fills you.

Love for Self

Unconditional love can be applied to any area of disturbance or hurt within yourself. Regardless of the issue, unconditional love will help. For example, if you're experiencing hurt feelings, apply love to the part of you who's hurting. If you're feeling afraid or stressed or frustrated, love the part of yourself who's feeling that way. If you find yourself judging someone, love the part of you who's judging—and love the person and love the judgment (then release it, as in "Chapter 3-5: Forgiveness," p. 61). If you despise the rain, love the part of you who's despising it. Unconditional love moves directly through any "shadows" within you (judgment, doubt, animosity, etc.) and brings transformative power into all that it finds.

Love for All Around You

Unconditional love is healing to others as well as to yourself. If you need proof, think of a time in the past when a kind word from someone else transformed hurt within you, or how you feel when your pet gazes at you with pure, unconditional love. Sometimes just a look of positive regard from someone else is all it takes to shift inner judgment, doubt, or darkness. A person doesn't even have to be aware of unconditional love in order for it to benefit them, nor do they even have to be nearby. Love can reach across distances similarly to light or a prayer (think of the way electricity can travel around the world in an instant).

Loving Through Challenges

You may notice parts of you that don't seem to be on board with your intention to love. For example, if someone else's actions led to anger within you, the part of you who feels angry may not feel very loving toward them. That's okay. In fact, it's better than okay because the beauty of love is its power to heal: when you allow love in, it suddenly brings to light those "not love" dynamics within you, and once you're mindful of them you can work through them (using techniques such as in "Part III: Haven-Building Toolkit," p. 35). And sometimes the love itself is enough to instantly shift those dynamics within you.

Whenever you find it challenging to choose unconditional love, here's a tip: choose it anyway. An intention is a very powerful thing.

When you can't seem to shift into unconditional love, try centering in soul (see "1. Center in Soul," p. 8). Soul is a place within you where unconditional love lives, so shifting in that direction will get you into the neighborhood. You can also call in the light, which tends to help everything ("Calling in the Light," p. 17).

Chapter 2-1: Stress and the Soul

If you're feeling resistance to unconditionally loving a particular person or group, you've found a great opportunity to practice seeing others as souls. Everyone is a soul living in a human body, and everyone is a being of unconditional love at their deepest level, even if your view of that is obscured at the moment. When you make the inner shift so that you're seeing others through the eyes of the soul that you are, you'll recognize soul within others ("Chapter 4-17: Seeing Others as Souls," p. 188).

You may notice particular situations in which you feel unable to shift into unconditional love no matter what you try. For example, if you're hesitating to move into unconditional love after you've crashed your car, it might help to take a step back and reframe the way you're viewing the situation. Number one, you're *alive* to consider how you feel about things. Number two, you don't know what life-changing opportunity or lesson could arise from it (see more in "Chapter 3-6: Reframing," p. 65). And you can may be able to come up with numbers three, four and five. But one great thing about unconditional love is that you don't *have* to talk yourself into it—you can simply choose it.

Love Always

The light of unconditional love is always burning within you like an eternal flame that never falters. You need only to choose into it. If you take away nothing else from this book, remember and practice this: Always love. Choose the unconditional love of soul as the place from which you experience the world.

Mind Mastery

If the highest level of your being is soul (which it is), then the ringmaster of the lower levels of your consciousness is your mind. And since you are a "higher being" who is soul, you are in charge of your mind because it's part of your consciousness over which you have complete domain. Therefore, you can use your mind as a tool so that it works for you rather than randomly or against you. And the mind can be a particularly beneficial tool during stressful times (as will be explained in more detail in "The Mind as a Stress Management Tool," p. 24).

One of the most effective uses of the mind is mindfulness, focusing your awareness on your thoughts and feelings in any moment. Within your own consciousness, awareness is power. That's because when you're paying attention to what's going on in your own consciousness, you're in a position to direct it in a way that works well for you.

The Mind as Energy in Motion

The mind—the mental, rational, thinking aspect of your consciousness—is constantly busy analyzing, generating thoughts, weighing decisions, keeping to-do lists, and a host of other activities. You'll find much of the mind's busy-work to be helpful, but you'll also notice some aspects that are counterproductive or even harmful. Limiting beliefs, self-defeating decisions, judgments of self or others, blaming, and even sarcasm will deteriorate and darken your inner environment.

Your mind is loaded with energy and filled with amazing resources. However, like an energetic puppy, if you don't channel the mind and guide it in productive and positive ways, it may channel its energy in destructive ways.

How to Become the Master of Your Mind

Becoming the master of your own mind means consciously making choices so that your mind serves you rather than rules you. The process of mind mastery involves first being aware of your mind (being mindful) and what it's doing in any moment (labelling, judging, assuming, rejecting, etc.), and then directing the mind in a way that better serves your best interests and higher purpose. We'll go into much more detail about techniques for various aspects of mind mastery in "Part III: Haven-Building Toolkit" (p. 35) and "Part IV: Quick-Fix Toolkit" (p. 161).

The Mind as a Stress-Management Tool

The mind makes an excellent tool for managing and coping with stress. When you're experiencing stress, you can put your mind to work in any direction you choose. You can assign it any task, such as:

- Identify the trigger that resulted in your stress reaction.
- Shift out of your stress reaction, such as by reframing the situation (see "Chapter 3-6: Reframing," p. 65).
- Figure out how to remove the emotional charge from the stress trigger.
- Discover how to remove, reduce, or avoid stress triggers in your environment (see "Chapter 4-27: Environmental Discernment," p. 206).
- Evaluate what would be most helpful for you right now (such as using one of the techniques in this book's toolkits).
- Assess what kind of assistance you need right now and where find it.
- Create a plan to deal with a particular challenge in order to reduce your stress level (see "Chapter 4-8: Preparation and Contingency Planning," p. 174).
- Imagine a time in the future when this stress will be gone (see "Chapter 4-6: Perspective," p. 171).

- Engage in a distracting activity as a temporary respite from stress (see "Chapter 4-21: Using Distraction," p. 196).
- Shift into a mindset that serves you better right now (see "Chapter 4-19: Thinking Locally," p. 192).
- Focus on the experience that you want instead of the stressful one (see "Chapter 3-16: Creating More of What You Want," p. 104).
- Inwardly repeat an affirmation or calming statement (see "Chapter 3-20: Affirmations," p. 120).
- Practice mindfulness as a means of staying present and stepping back from your stress reaction (see "Chapter 4-11: Observing Your Thoughts," p. 181).
- Identify ways to take exquisite care of yourself right now.

Working Your Process

Stress is a signal that you have an opportunity to improve the way you're reacting to or handling something. In other words, stress indicates one or more issues within yourself that need your attention. Because working through an issue involves going through a process, you might think of this as "working your process." (It really doesn't matter what you call it, as long as you *do* it.) "Working your process" means completing whatever inner work is necessary to resolve your issue, which then usually results in reducing stress, illuminating inner areas of darkness, healing, enhancing well-being, and experiencing profound peace and greater alignment with soul. Each issue resolved is one step in your process, and each step takes you forward and upward. "Chapter 2-2: Using the Techniques in This Book" (p. 27) will help you explore how you can use the techniques in this book to work your process.

Rules of Stress Management

When working with stress reactions within yourself, keep in mind these rules for dealing with stress effectively:

- First, always call in the light (see "Calling in the Light," p. 17).
- Remember that you are a soul walking through this human experience.
- Love everything: love the part of you that's stressed, afraid, angry, or confused, and love others involved, even if you don't like them (see "Applying Love," p. 20).
- Practice acceptance of what is, even if you don't like it or you plan to change it (see "Chapter 3-2: Acceptance," p. 43).

- If you find yourself judging yourself or others, release the judgments (see "Chapter 3-5: Forgiveness," p. 61).
- Practice mindfulness and stay present in the moment.
- Direct your focus. Whatever you're choosing to focus on, focus on that. Even if you're choosing to distract yourself, focus on that.
- Be your own champion. Cheer yourself on. Own the fact that you are amazing. If you don't feel amazing, own it anyway.
- In relating to others, always look for win-win situations—ones that benefit both you and others involved.
- Don't make any major decisions when experiencing stress, if you can help it. It's okay to decide not to decide. Delay a decision until the latest possible time, when you may be feeling more clarity. In the meantime you can only gain more information, not less (see "Chapter 3-14: Decision Making," p. 95).
- Remember that "this too shall pass."
- I also strongly encourage you to make a commitment to yourself and to honoring your own process by following the steps in "Committing to Soul" (p. 11), "Oath to Self" (p. 28), and "Taking Personal Responsibility" (p. 28).

Chapter 2-2

Using the Techniques in This Book

In This Chapter:
Lay the Groundwork First 27
How to Work with the Techniques 28

In this chapter, you'll learn the important steps to take before using the techniques in this book, and then how to get started with the techniques. The techniques are divided into two toolkits, the first focusing on deeper transformational stress relief for the long-term, and the second focusing on quick fixes for stress:

- **HAVEN-BUILDING TOOLKIT (p. 35)**—A collection of powerful, transformative techniques to facilitate personal growth and healing. You can use these techniques to build a strong, soul-centered haven within yourself to help you weather any storm life brings. They can be applied in any area of your life to elevate your consciousness and facilitate inner peace, while also particularly effective for reducing stress reactions to both inner and external stress triggers.
- **QUICK-FIX TOOLKIT (p. 161)**—Techniques that can be used instantly in any moment you're experiencing stress, distress, or disturbance. They offer an umbrella in any storm by creating an immediate shift within your consciousness. In most cases, these techniques offer a temporary respite from stress that may or may not last longer-term.

Lay the Groundwork First

Before you begin using the techniques, you'll need to prepare by taking the steps in the next two sections.

Oath to Self

Stress or crisis in your life provides an opportunity for exquisite self-care. Your attitude toward yourself can make all the difference in your inner experience and the quality of inner transformation and healing. So, before beginning any work with yourself, make this personal oath to yourself:

- I intend to use all experiences for my own learning, growth, and upliftment.
- I intend to use what works well for me and let go of the rest.
- I intend to love myself and others unconditionally.
- I commit to being gentle with myself and with others.
- I commit to taking care of myself, which also better enables me to help others.

Taking Personal Responsibility

As always, be responsible when working through issues: always work in a way that's safe for yourself and for anyone else around you, and if you feel unable to handle something, seek help from a mental health professional. (For more about personal responsibility, see "Chapter 3-3: Responsibility," p. 46.)

How to Work with the Techniques

Before beginning any technique, always call in the light. You can do this by inwardly saying, "I ask for the light to fill, surround, and protect me for the highest good of all concerned" (see more in "How to Call in the Light," p. 18). Think of this as the very important first step in every technique.

You can use any of this book's techniques in any order. Regardless of which technique you begin with, any issues within you that are ready to be addressed will likely come forward during the process if you hold the intention to work through your issues, uplift your consciousness, and heal.

Keep in mind that some of these techniques may seem deceptively simple. However, even a very basic technique can lead to a process of profound inner transformation and healing. In fact, some of the most powerful techniques are very simple ones.

Reading through a technique will tell you very little about how helpful the technique will be for you. The proof is in using it. You'll need to actually apply a technique and complete the process yourself to discover its benefits, and you may be surprised at the depth and quality of inner transformation you experience.

For some of these techniques, repetition and consistency over time is key, and their benefits are cumulative (such as "Chapter 3-9: Transforming

Negative Self-Talk," p. 75, "Chapter 3-16: Creating More of What You Want," p. 104, "Chapter 3-18: Spiritual Exercises," p. 114, "Chapter 3-20: Affirmations," p. 120, and "Chapter 3-21: Meditation," p. 124).

Core Techniques

The first 17 techniques in "Part III: Haven-Building Toolkit" (p. 35) are the core techniques for building a strong, soul-centered inner haven through transforming the "not peace" dynamics that keep you focused in the lower levels and can obstruct your experience of soul. By practicing these 17 techniques, you'll also build skills that are essential for a happier and more peaceful relationship with yourself and the world:

- Chapter 3-1: Working Through an Issue (p. 38)
- Chapter 3-2: Acceptance (p. 43)
- Chapter 3-3: Responsibility" (p. 46)
- Chapter 3-4: Processing Emotions (p. 58)
- Chapter 3-5: Forgiveness (p. 61)
- Chapter 3-6: Reframing (p. 65)
- Chapter 3-7: Transforming Beliefs (p. 68)
- Chapter 3-8: Setting Intentions (p. 71)
- Chapter 3-9: Transforming Negative Self-Talk (p. 75)
- Chapter 3-10: Exploring Projections (p. 78)
- Chapter 3-11: Revisiting Past Decisions (p. 85)
- Chapter 3-12: Completing Unfinished Business (p. 87)
- Chapter 3-13: Renegotiating Outdated Agreements (p. 90)
- Chapter 3-14: Decision Making (p. 95)
- Chapter 3-15: Leaning Into Your Strengths (p. 99)
- Chapter 3-16: Creating More of What You Want (p. 104)
- Chapter 3-17: Deepening Your Spirituality (p. 110)

Getting Started

The following sections provide some ideas for how to get started when applying the techniques.

Start with What Is Present

One way to work with these techniques is to begin with whatever issue is most present for you in this moment. Follow the steps in "Chapter 3-1: Working Through an Issue" (p. 38) and then supplement that process with other techniques based on whatever else arises during that process. For example, if you discover that you're judging yourself in a certain way, release that judgment using "Chapter 3-5: Forgiveness" (p. 61). If your process reveals a self-defeating belief, transform it using "Chapter 3-7: Transforming Beliefs" (p. 68). Continue working with various techniques until your process feels complete—until you feel at peace and you are not aware of any other inner issues needing your attention.

Start with What Is Most Stressful

Another approach is to start with whatever you consider most stressful right now. Examine the stressful situation and pick it apart until you find the underlying stress trigger. (If you need more clarity, try the exercise in "Chapter 3-22: Free-Form Writing," p. 127, and focus your writing on the topic of the underlying triggers in this stressful situation.) Then take steps to disarm the trigger by transforming the part of yourself that's reacting when you encounter or think of that trigger. How you'll disarm it depends on the nature of the trigger (for examples, see "Choosing Techniques," p. 31, and "Part V: Quick Reference," p. 211).

Once you've removed the trigger's emotional charge and your inner process feels complete, consider what (if any) external actions you'll take to change the trigger or reduce its effects on you—such as delegating some of the items on your to-do list or asking to be relocated away from a coworker whom you find particularly challenging.

Follow Your Intuition (Sometimes)

Usually, following your intuition would be a great strategy for selecting a technique to work with. However, when you're in a stressed state of mind or heightened state of emotion, intuition is often obscured. If you attempt to access your intuition when you're mentally or emotionally stressed, you're more likely to tap into your subconscious fears, hopes, or other dynamics. This isn't to say that you should avoid following your intuition, but rather be aware of the disruptive effect of stress on your ability to access intuition.

Intuition tends to come forward quietly and neutrally when you're feeling calm and relaxed. More specifically, you might notice heightened intuition when you're centered in soul (see "The Steps for Getting to Soul," p. 7), such as after doing spiritual exercises (see "Chapter 3-18: Spiritual Exercises," p. 114). Some people notice that intuitive insights tend to show up often when taking a shower, spending time in nature, or engaging in an easy activity that leaves the consciousness free to roam (such as doing housework or going for a walk).

Learning to discern intuition from other factors in your consciousness (such as fears, hopes, and desires) is a process. As you pay attention to how you experience your own intuitive knowing, you can begin to recognize the difference between your intuition and other internal dynamics such as emotions, thoughts, and imaginings. Each internal factor feels different

CHAPTER 2-2: USING THE TECHNIQUES IN THIS BOOK

once you learn to discern among them—although the differences can be very subtle.

It can take years to develop the ability to tap into your intuition at will, quickly and accurately. However, as you practice you should notice improvements over time. You might want to enhance your intuitive skills through intuition exercises, many of which can be found online and in books.

One way to practice recognizing intuition is to create an intuition notebook in which you track your insights that you believe come from your intuition. For each insight you experience, describe what the inner experience felt like; how you felt mentally, emotionally, and physically; what you were thinking or talking about just before the intuition showed up; and circumstances such as what you were doing, where you were, and so on. Then check your insight against reality (as is feasible) and note how accurate each insight turned out to be, and whether it seemed to actually be based on intuition or perhaps just fear, imagination, desire, or some other factor. Tracking these details gives you a chance to practice accessing intuition and discerning your intuition from other inner factors, and it may also point out the kinds of situations in which your intuition tends to be more active or more available to you.

Mind Your Resistance
Sometimes the technique to which you feel the greatest resistance is actually the one that would be most helpful. This could be because your issue is "kicking up a dust storm" within you because you fear the discomfort that working through the issue might involve. So if a certain technique jumps out and you have a strong reaction such as, "No, definitely not that one!", then pay attention. You may want to consider whether that is exactly the technique that would help most. Sometimes a certain technique can help by "stirring up" an issue further so you can see it and its underlying dynamics more clearly. In any case, you can always begin the process and see how it goes, and then switch to another technique if this one doesn't seem to fit.

Choosing Techniques
Here are some examples of situations that might prompt you to use particular techniques in "Part III: Haven-Building Toolkit" (p. 35):

- If something about a situation, a person, or yourself bothers you, start with accepting that it is the way it is, independent of whether you don't like it or plan to change it ("Chapter 3-2: Acceptance," p. 43).

PART II: SOUL-CENTERED STRESS MANAGEMENT

- If you find yourself reacting in a negative way to a person or situation, acknowledge your responsibility for your own reactions and transform them ("Chapter 3-3: Responsibility," p. 46).
- If you're experiencing strong emotion, such as in reaction to a stress trigger or if you're feeling sad or hurt, process through your feelings to remove the emotional charge ("Chapter 3-4: Processing Emotions," p. 58).
- If you're judging yourself or someone else as wrong or bad, release your judgments ("Chapter 3-5: Forgiveness," p. 61).
- If you notice that you're labelling a situation as "good" or "bad," try reframing it in a way that serves you better ("Chapter 3-6: Reframing," p. 65).
- If you notice you have a belief that's self-defeating or outdated (such as "I can never do anything right"), release and replace it ("Chapter 3-7: Transforming Beliefs," p. 68).
- If you want to make a change within yourself or within your areas of responsibility, set an intention to jumpstart and reinforce the change over time ("Chapter 3-8: Setting Intentions," p. 71).
- If you're feeling restricted or overwhelmed in your day-to-day life, consider whether you're limiting yourself by outdated decisions ("Chapter 3-11: Revisiting Past Decisions," p. 85) or beliefs ("Chapter 3-7: Transforming Beliefs," p. 68), or if you've taken on a responsibility that isn't yours ("Chapter 3-3: Responsibility," p. 46).
- If the words you're telling yourself in your head bring you down or lead to frustration or sadness, transform your style of inner dialogue with yourself ("Chapter 3-9: Transforming Negative Self-Talk," p. 75).
- If you feel incomplete about anything, such as a commitment to self or others or something that in the past you told yourself you'd do sometime, find a way to reach closure with it somehow ("Chapter 3-12: Completing Unfinished Business," p. 87).
- If you're not happy with your life or a certain aspect of it, focus on what experience you'd like instead and put your energy toward creating that ("Chapter 3-16: Creating More of What You Want," p. 104, "Chapter 3-8: Setting Intentions," p. 71, "Chapter 3-20: Affirmations," p. 120).
- If your mind feels cluttered or you're experiencing mental overwhelm, explore techniques that clarify, clear, and organize your consciousness ("Chapter 3-22: Free-Form Writing," p. 127, "Chapter 3-23: Writing a Shred Letter," p. 132, "Chapter 3-24: Mental Clean-Sweep," p. 135).
- If you have thoughts or feelings that remain unspoken or find yourself imagining a hypothetical conversation over and over, express them in

Chapter 2-2: Using the Techniques in This Book

a safe way to help you reach closure ("Chapter 3-23: Writing a Shred Letter," p. 132).
- If you're experiencing upset or distress (frustration, fear, etc.) but can't quite identify what's bothering you, try an open-ended process that prompts an outward flow from your subconscious mind ("Chapter 3-22: Free-Form Writing," p. 127, "Chapter 3-23: Writing a Shred Letter," p. 132, "Chapter 3-26: Dream Interpretation," p. 144).
- If you're feeling easily distracted or having trouble focusing, a technique that centers you may help ("Chapter 3-18: Spiritual Exercises," p. 114, "Chapter 3-21: Meditation," p. 124, "Chapter 4-15: Visualization," p. 185, "Chapter 3-19: Rainbow Visualization," p. 118).
- If you tend to experience stress when you spend time with certain people, perhaps it's time to reevaluate your social interaction choices ("Chapter 4-26: Social Discernment," p. 204).

For a list of questions to ask yourself when choosing which technique to use, see "Part V: Quick Reference" (p. 211).

PART III

HAVEN-BUILDING TOOLKIT

About This Toolkit

This toolkit includes powerful techniques for facilitating your process of centering your awareness more directly in soul and removing obstacles to experiencing soul. In addition, the first 17 are "core techniques," each of which builds an essential skill for relating to yourself and the world in a soul-centered way. You can use this toolkit to build a strong, soul-centered haven within yourself to help you weather any storm life may bring.

Before using these techniques, be sure you've read "Chapter 2-2: Using the Techniques in This Book" (p. 27).

Chapter 3-1
Working Through an Issue

This chapter introduces a basic process for working through an issue. An issue is anything within yourself that causes you disturbance or keeps you from experiencing peace. The three-step process presented here can be very effective for many issues that arise. However, resolving a larger issue or one with more extensive underlying dynamics may require further processing using additional techniques. I suggest starting with this process and then adding other techniques in this book as needed (such as "Chapter 3-5: Forgiveness," p. 61, or "Chapter 3-6: Reframing," p. 65).

Benefits

The process of working through issues is the cornerstone of personal growth and inner healing. Every issue you work through transforms an area within your consciousness from "not peace" to peace, removing "darkness" from that area and allowing it to be filled with peaceful light. In other words, working through an issue reduces stress and creates more peace within you.

Working through your issues is liberating, healing, uplifting, and empowering. Each issue you resolve allows the authentic you to come forward even more, enabling you to experience soul more directly and express more of who you truly are.

Each technique you apply while working through an issue offers its own specific benefits. For example, releasing judgments can remove self-limitations and can open you to new opportunities ("Chapter 3-5: Forgiveness," p. 61). Reframing empowers you to interpret your experiences in a way that works *for* you rather than against you. Setting an intention aligns and commits your entire consciousness in a direction of your choosing. For more about specific benefits, see the chapters for each technique.

CHAPTER 3-1: WORKING THROUGH AN ISSUE

The Process

This section presents three basic steps for working through an issue. Before you begin, always call in the light (see "Calling in the Light," p. 17). I recommend also setting intentions for your process, such as "I intend to take complete responsibility for any reactions and judgments I may have during this process" and "I intend to love myself unconditionally throughout this process" (see "Chapter 3-8: Setting Intentions," p. 71).

1. Express Your Current Emotions

Release emotions associated with the issue by experiencing them (safely)—allowing yourself to feel them—thereby getting them out of your system.

Processing through any emotions involved with the issue will allow you to then get to the heart of the issue (underlying those emotions) so you can resolve it. Emotions include anger, fear, sadness, guilt, jealousy, and resentment, among many others. You can process through emotions and release them from your system by allowing yourself to experience them, allowing them to flow and then dissipate. One way to think of emotions is as bits of energy that flow out of you as you feel or express them.

Because emotions often "piggyback on top of" an issue, they can obscure the issue until you have gotten them out of your system. Emotions can also "lock in" an issue, making it impossible to resolve before the emotions have been fully expressed. For example, you might still be judging yourself (a mental dynamic) for missing the winning shot years ago that would have clinched your high school basketball championship. On top of that self-judgment you've piled years of anger (an emotional dynamic), which has further entrenched and reinforced the self-judgment. So, processing through that anger first will clear the way to then release the judgment. (This concept of processing emotions before resolving the issue may not make sense to you yet, but it will when you're trying to release a mental dynamic that's been "locked in" by emotion and the dynamic won't release. You'll get the hang of this, and it will begin to come naturally.)

One sign of emotional maturity is being able to process your emotions without dumping them on others. **Be sure you express your emotions in a safe way that will not hurt yourself or others,** such as through free-form writing or a shred letter (see instructions in "Chapter 3-22: Free-Form Writing," p. 127, and "Chapter 3-23: Writing a Shred Letter," p. 132). You can also express them inwardly or in a prayer, or out loud if you have privacy. Start by expressing how you feel beginning with the words "I feel..." (such as "I feel angry..." or "I feel really frustrated...") and then use words to express whatever you're feeling within you at the moment. Don't judge your feelings. (They're going to be gone in a moment, anyway.) Just keep those feelings flowing in a safe way until there are no more, they've all faded away, and the process feels complete. If you can't express your emotions in a way that's safe for you and for others around you, then stop immediately and ask for support from a mental health professional to support you in the safe expression of your emotion.

In some cases, simply expressing your emotions can resolve the issue, which means you don't need to continue to the next step if you already feel complete and the issue has been resolved.

(You can read more in-depth about expressing emotions in "Chapter 3-4: Processing Emotions," p. 58.)

2. Make Inner Adjustments

Transform the inner dynamics that are contributing to the issue, and make decisions about any changes you want to make.

If expressing your emotions did not completely resolve your issue, then it's time to explore and make adjustments to the underlying dynamics that are contributing to the issue. Often these dynamics involve holding onto negativity or self-limitation—such as judgments, irrational or outdated beliefs, or negative self-talk. You can transform these dynamics by first becoming aware of them and then taking steps to shift or release them.

To resolve an issue—in order for real healing to happen—you must deal with all of the emotional and mental dynamics involved in the issue. If more emotions come up during this step, express them as described in Step 1 and then return to this step.

3. Take External Action

Take steps in your life around you, such as in your relationships, career, finances, or environment.

Depending on the particular issue, you may decide that in order to resolve it you need to take external action in addition to any internal adjustments you made in Step 2. You may choose to take steps or make an external change in your life, such as apologizing to a friend, thanking your mother, or modifying your daily routine. You might also decide you want to take external action to support any internal adjustments you made in Step 2, such as changing your life direction or creating a physical touchstone to remind you of a new self-supporting belief. Any actions you take are completely up to you. Remember that you alone are responsible for your actions and their consequences, so use your best judgment and act from a place of goodwill toward yourself and others.

Chapter 3-1: Working Through an Issue

Examples

Example A

Here's an example of working through an issue involving feeling wronged by someone in the past who borrowed money and then refused to pay it back, and you've been judging that person. Holding onto that judgment means carrying around all that hurt, anger, pain, and resentment within yourself in perpetuity until you release the judgment. The judgment is creating a negative area within your consciousness that darkens and weighs you down. It also keeps you tied to the past by effectively "locking in" that past "wrong" action within you, which in turn keeps you from letting go of the past and moving on (see more in "Chapter 3-5: Forgiveness," p. 61). In this example, you follow the three steps just described to work through the issue:

1. **Express Your Current Emotions**—You write a shred letter ("Chapter 3-23: Writing a Shred Letter," p. 132) in which you express how you feel about this past action, continuing until you feel you've had your say and the emotional charge has subsided.
2. **Make Inner Adjustment**—You accept that you loaned money and didn't get it back, and that you very well may never get it back ("Chapter 3-2: Acceptance," p. 43). You release the judgment you've been holding against that person as a "bad" person for what he did, acknowledging that you haven't walked in his shoes and don't know exactly what was going on in his consciousness when he took the action he did (see "Chapter 3-5: Forgiveness," p. 61). You also release your judgment of yourself for holding onto resentment so long. Releasing these judgments benefits you because they've been "living inside" your head creating negativity there. You also reevaluate a past decision you made to always help financially whenever anyone needs it, and you replace it with a new decision to either put a loan agreement in writing clearly or give the money freely with no expectation to be repaid ("Chapter 3-11: Revisiting Past Decisions," p. 85).
3. **Take External Action**—You consider possible actions such as suing the person to get the money back (which you decide is not worth your time) or paying a lawyer to write a letter (which you decide would cost more than you're willing to pay). You decide instead to ask the person again nicely, especially since you were pretty angry when you talked to him about before. You plan to talk about the original agreement as you understood it, and then listen to what he

has to say. You also decide that if he still refuses to pay you back, you are willing to let the matter go, consider the money a gift, and consider this a lesson learned. You pick up the phone and call him.

Example B

Another type of issue involves beliefs within your consciousness that are outdated, irrational, or self-defeating in some way. You can release such a belief and replace it with an updated belief that works well and rings true for you now (see "Chapter 3-7: Transforming Beliefs," p. 68).

An example of this kind of issue would be experiencing stress as a result of feeling like you always have to "do more" and "be more" in order to feel good about yourself. You've stretched yourself thin trying to do everything and be everything you think you should do and be. You complete the steps for working through an issue this way:

1. **Express Your Current Emotions**—Using free-form writing ("Chapter 3-22: Free-Form Writing," p. 127), you unload all of your frustration about constantly trying to do more and be more. As you write, you note a few judgments and beliefs to work on in Step 2, and then you keep writing until there's nothing left to say and you're feeling more neutral.
2. **Make Inner Adjustment**—You release judgments of yourself that came up in Step 1, including "I release the judgment of myself as not enough as I am" and "I release the judgment of myself as a bad for not being better than I am" (see "Chapter 3-5: Forgiveness," p. 61). You then release self-defeating beliefs, including "I release the belief that I need to prove myself in order to be accepted by others" and "I release the belief that my only value is in my actions that benefit others." You also revisit a decision you made a long time ago to always put others' needs above yours, and you replace it with a new decision to make sure your needs are met so you can then help others ("Chapter 3-11: Revisiting Past Decisions," p. 85).
3. **Take External Action**—To reinforce your new decision, you create an affirmation of "I am caring for myself with patience and kindness," and you post it on sticky notes around the house where you'll see it often. You also commit to checking in with yourself twice a day to assess any unmet needs and how to meet them.

Chapter 3-2

Acceptance

Acceptance means admitting to yourself that something *is the way it is* right now, or *was the way it was* in the past. In other words, acceptance means acknowledging that right now in this moment, a certain thing (you, someone else, a situation) is as it is, or was as it was—regardless of whether it is the way you want it to be or was the way you wanted it to be, or whether you might act to change it in the future.

For example, if you're out of money, you can choose to accept that you don't have any money right now, even if you you're not happy about it and even if you plan to change that situation. Accepting that you're low on funds doesn't mean you're agreeing that you like being that way or that you'll always be that way. Acceptance simply means that you're acknowledging to yourself that right now you don't have any money. Your acceptance of that fact enables you to break out of current patterns such as denial ("I really don't have money problems"), escapism ("I don't have money problems if I distract myself from that fact"), excuses ("I only spent all my money because my favorite store was having a big sale"), and wallowing in misery ("Being without money is so awful—I'm too upset to do anything but watch TV all day"). Acceptance interrupts those patterns and enables you to start fresh in finding a path to a better situation.

Likewise, you can choose to accept something that happened in the past, such as the fact that you dented your car when you backed into a telephone pole. Accepting that you hit the telephone pole doesn't place blame or judgment on you. Acceptance simply means you are acknowledging to yourself, "I did it," which allows you to move immediately into "…and so, what next?" Perhaps next you will decide to release your judgment against yourself as a "bad" person for having hit the pole, set an intention to focus more on your surroundings when driving, and get started today setting aside money for your car repair.

Benefits

Acceptance can bring great peace immediately. Once you accept that something is the way it is (or was the way it was), you may be surprised how much energy you were expending by fighting against it, denying it, thinking about it, or trying to avoid thinking about it. You may suddenly feel a load lift off of you when you stop fighting what is, or what was.

Once you accept something, often you can see the situation more clearly. You may be less afraid to look at and explore the situation than when you were fighting or avoiding it, and that deeper understanding of the situation is important to help you decide what your next step will be.

Accepting something can immediately shift your awareness into the actual issue and its underlying dynamics, such as judgments, guilt, blame, or self-defeating patterns of denial or excuses. This awareness then enables you to work through and shift them (see more in "Chapter 3-1: Working Through an Issue," p. 38).

When you accept, you to move into the mode of "What's next?" rather than remaining hung up in the past, whether it's the distant past or the past of just a few minutes ago. Acceptance moves you into the now. When you accept, you are accepting *right now,* in the moment.

Acceptance creates a clear space with you, from which you can more easily move forward and change things. Although you accept something, you may still not be happy about it and want to change it—which is fine. However, in order to change something, you must start from the way it is *right now* and make changes from this point forward. In any moment, all you have is now. The first step is acceptance, and then you move forward from there.

The Process

The process of acceptance has only one step: Say inwardly or outwardly, "I accept..." and then describe what you're accepting right now, in the moment. Remember that by accepting something, you don't necessarily have to like it, agree with it, or want it to stay the way it is. You are merely confirming that something *is* or *was,* and you still have the ability to change it or change the way you relate to it.

Because acceptance is often the first step of working through an issue or changing the way you relate to a situation, you may choose to follow it up with additional steps. For example, if you're feeling strong emotions, you might process through them using "Chapter 3-4: Processing Emotions" (p. 58). To work through an issue, you might follow the steps in

CHAPTER 3-2: ACCEPTANCE

"Chapter 3-1: Working Through an Issue" (p. 38). If you'd like to change how you relate to a situation, see "Chapter 3-6: Reframing" (p. 65).

Examples

Here are some examples of acceptance statements:
- "I accept that it is hot outside today."
- "I accept that I arrived late to work again this morning."
- "I accept that the professor marked a grade of C on my homework."
- "I accept that the stoplight is red right now."
- "I accept that my parents cancelled their plans to visit me."

Chapter 3-3
Responsibility

How you relate to responsibility depends a lot on the wording you use in your inner dialogue with yourself. Viewing a responsibility as something that "you have to do" or "someone is forcing you to do" implies giving your power over to some authority who's "making" you be responsible. An alternative way to view responsibility is as "personal power." When you're choosing to be responsible for something (or for yourself), you're placing yourself in the powerful position of overseer and decision maker for that responsibility. Being responsible also implies freedom to choose how and when you handle that responsibility, meaning you get to be in control. So choosing responsibility means having true power within yourself and in your life.

When you accept a responsibility as your own you're actually *deciding* to take charge of it, *setting an intention* to continue being in charge until the responsibility ends, and *agreeing* to following it through. This triple-whammy is indeed a potent combination that aligns and activates your inner resources toward a desired result (see also "Chapter 3-14: Decision Making," p. 95, "Chapter 3-8: Setting Intentions," p. 71, and "Chapter 3-13: Renegotiating Outdated Agreements," p. 90). You can use this trio to your advantage by applying responsibility as a tool in creating the quality of life and experience you desire.

In this chapter we'll consider four main types of responsibilities in daily life: for self, for others, in relationships and interactions, and in agreements. Some of these are responsibilities you've agreed to take on, while others are intrinsic to existence as a human being—and some of which you may not have yet acknowledged but that can improve your life magnificently. When you learn to view responsibility as empowerment, your life can suddenly become more meaningful and pleasant. In the following sections, we'll examine in greater detail the benefits and "how to's" of this perspective on responsibility.

CHAPTER 3-3: RESPONSIBILITY

Responsibility for Self

As human beings, we all have certain responsibilities for ourselves. For example, each of us is responsible for making sure our basic physical needs are met for air, food, water, shelter, and so on (unless we're incapable of that for some reason). But our self-responsibilities extend much further. You (like every human) are also responsible for overseeing all areas of your own consciousness and aspects of your life, including these primary ones:

- Your physical, mental, and emotional well-being.
- Your actions and their results and consequences.
- Your role in creating or allowing a particular situation or result.
- Your consciousness, including what you do and don't allow to take root or persist within it (see more in "Managing Your Thoughts," p. 47).
- Your reactions—such as to external events, people, your own thoughts, or other things that show up within your consciousness (see more in "Owning Your Reactions," p. 48).
- Working through your own issues in a way that's loving toward yourself and others (see "Lay the Groundwork First," p. 27, and "Chapter 3-1: Working Through an Issue," p. 38).

If you aren't aware that you have all of these responsibilities, don't worry—you're not the only one. Most of us weren't taught as children how to work through our own issues (releasing judgments, evaluating beliefs, etc.). Some of us may have heard the idea that "You may not be able to control events in your life, but you can control your reaction to them." However, we can't be expected to know how to change our reactions if we don't have the understanding or the tools to do so. This book fills that void with techniques to clarify and simplify meeting your responsibilities to yourself (especially the first 17 techniques in "Part III: Haven-Building Toolkit," p. 35).

Next, let's take a closer look at two of the areas of self-responsibility that can make a huge difference within your own consciousness: managing your thoughts and owning your reactions.

Managing Your Thoughts

Imagine you're walking along on a path and you notice a smooth stone lying on the ground. It's just a stone—not good or bad or meaningful—just a chunk of rock. What you do with the stone is what gives it meaning and gives it power in your mind:

- You could declare it an obstacle and kick it out of the way.
- You could see the stone as a source of fun and skip it across a pond.

- You could marvel at its beautiful texture and color, and move on.
- You could examine it under a microscope to expand your understanding of it.
- You could even decide it has magical powers and build a whole belief system around it.
- You could just ignore it and keep walking.

It's the same with thoughts. When a thought comes into your mind, it's just a thought. You can choose what you do with it. Like the rock, you can pick it up and do something with it, or not. You can use it to weigh yourself down, perhaps with guilt or judgment. You can examine it to see what value it may have. You can ignore it, let it pass, and say, "Next!"

You may not be in control of what thoughts pop into your mind, but you're absolutely in charge of what you do with them. You decide what thoughts you dwell on, buy into, give power to, act on, transform, or let go of. You can choose to embrace only thoughts that serve you well, celebrate yourself and others, and bring out your best.

Owning Your Reactions

You are responsible for your reactions to people, situations, and events. No one else is creating or causing your reactions—others don't have that kind of power over you. There is no such thing as, "It's your fault I'm in a bad mood." Instead, consider how you're choosing to interpret a situation in a way that perpetuates a bad mood within yourself. There is no such thing as, "You made me jealous." Instead, you are choosing to react to an external event by allowing jealousy or insecurity to rule within yourself. You—and only you—have the power and the control over your reactions. You create, allow, or veto every reaction within your consciousness.

With this realization comes power, but also responsibility. If no one can actually *make* you angry, then all of that anger is created within you, by you. It's yours. It really has nothing to do with the other person—they were just a trigger for you. What you're experiencing is *your reaction,* and your reaction belongs to you. And that means you can take charge of it and you can change it. Here are some tips:

- Practice taking responsibility for your reactions. When you hear yourself giving your power away by thinking "It's his fault," or "She makes me so angry!", hear a bell going off in your head reminding you that you're experiencing a reaction, you're in charge of it, and you can change it.

- When drama shows up within you, become the director of your inner story and make it a positive one in which you're the hero who's creating win-win situations.
- Recognize that no one has the power to make you angry, resentful, or anything else. You can't change other people, but you can change your reactions to them. You are in charge of you.

Responsibility for Others

Many of us have responsibility for others. For example, if you have a child, then you have responsibility for that child and his or her well-being. The same is true if you have a pet. You may also have made a commitment to take care of someone else, such as a parent, relative, or neighbor who needs assistance. There are many ways and situations in which we choose to take responsibility for others, including on physical, mental, emotional, financial, or other levels.

However, sometimes we try to take responsibility for someone else in a way that crosses their boundaries. For example, if you try to tell another person (for whom you're not directly responsible) what to believe, how to act, or how to go about daily life when they haven't asked for your input, you're entering into an area that is not your responsibility and is therefore not up to you. You can ask if they'd like your input, but they have the right to say "no."

Likewise, sometimes we try to take responsibility for someone in a way that deprives that person of taking responsibility for themselves. For instance, if a friend repeatedly runs up their credit card bills and you rescue him by paying the bills, you're actually "rescuing" him from learning to take responsibility for his own finances (which isn't a favor in the long run).

You're not responsible for others for whom you're not a parent, caretaker, or other agreed-upon helper. You may *choose* to help them if they need and want help, or you may choose to occasionally do a kind deed, but you're not *responsible* for their well-being, opinions, beliefs, stress, and so on. Every adult is in charge of their own domain. The flip side of this is that when you're not responsible for someone else, you don't have to carry that weight of responsibility on your shoulders—which makes things a lot lighter on you.

When you have responsibilities to others who depend on you, it's so important to take those seriously. This is because, unlike a responsibility to yourself, neglecting a responsibility for another person means that they're the ones who suffer the consequences. So even when you don't particularly want or like handling these responsibilities, you must honor your agreements unless and until you're able to renegotiate them or make other arrangements (for example, if your daughter needs help with social studies and you despise the subject, you might arrange for a tutor to help her).

Responsibility in Relationships and Interactions

We all have responsibilities within the context of relationships, including ongoing relationships as well as simple interactions with strangers in our daily lives. For example, when encountering a person you don't know, you have a responsibility for at least a basic sense of humanity, ideally expanding to include the following responsibilities:

- Goodwill.
- Open-mindedness.
- Respect.
- Acceptance of them as a person ("Chapter 3-2: Acceptance," p. 43).
- Acknowledging them as a beautiful soul ("Chapter 4-17: Seeing Others as Souls," p. 188).

In your relationships with family members, friends, or coworkers you have that same set of responsibilities, plus additional responsibilities in terms of how you participate in that relationship ongoing, such as:

- Openness, honesty, kindness, and choosing your words wisely.
- Listening well and asking for clarification when needed.
- Consideration of the other person's needs and feelings, as well as your own.
- Expressing your own feelings, including when something in the relationship isn't working well for you.
- Your role in the shared responsibility of creating and maintaining a healthy relationship.
- Fulfilling any agreements you've made in the context of that relationship (such as agreeing to professional behavior at work or marriage vows in a marriage).
- Acknowledging that you're responsible for your own reactions.
- Respecting the other person's boundaries and personal process, and speaking up if you feel they're intruding into yours.

The more responsibility you take in relationships with others, the higher the quality of the relationship and interactions within it. Returning to the idea of responsibility as empowerment discussed at the beginning of this chapter, when you manage your responsibility in a relationship you empower the relationship to elevate to a higher-level experience. However, neglecting your responsibility within a relationship can cause it to deteriorate.

In any relationship or interaction, you are not responsible for the other person's thoughts, opinions, or reactions. This means those dynamics are part of that person's domain rather than yours, and you can't control them. However, you can control whether and how you choose to interact with that person. For example, if you have good reason to expect that interacting with a certain person will lead to an experience you don't want, such as unpleasant attitude or unwelcome opinions, you can take steps to avoid it (such as by choosing not to interact with that person, having a third person present, or waiting until you're both calm).

Responsibility for Agreements

Responsibilities involving agreements or commitments to complete certain tasks are very familiar to most of us. These responsibilities include agreements you've made verbally (such as "I'll take out the garbage every week") and agreements you've implied (such as by consistently taking the garbage each week, although words of agreement were never spoken).

This type of responsibility includes all sorts of promises, commitments, contracts, and other agreements we make to others and to ourselves. Agreements fill our daily lives. You've probably created a great number of agreements for which you're responsible, from rental contracts to promising yourself you'll brush your teeth twice a day.

If you've taken on responsibility for something to which you never agreed, or for something to which you agreed but now want to let go of, you may want to take a closer look at it to renegotiate or otherwise divest yourself of that responsibility. Sometimes an agreement you've made with yourself doesn't serve your best interests and can actually limit you, such as agreeing that you'll never rest until you achieve "perfection." (You can read much more about this type of responsibility and how to reevaluate agreements that no longer serve you in "Chapter 3-13: Renegotiating Outdated Agreements," p. 90.)

Responsibility as a Tool for Stress

When you're stressed about something, a great question to ask yourself is, "Is it mine?" In other words, "Is this *my* responsibility, or is this something that *requires my* attention, involvement, or energy?" Let's break down this question further:

- "Is this *my* responsibility?"—Have I agreed to this responsibility, or do I want to agree to take it on as mine?
- "Is this something that *requires* my attention?"—Is it absolutely necessary for me to invest my time, attention, and energy on this?
- "Is this something that requires *my* attention?"—Do I have to be the one to handle this? Is someone else already working on handling this (or will be), and am I willing to let them take care of it (or can I get to the point where I'm willing to)?

Your energy, time, state of mind, and health are precious enough that you'd be wise to scrutinize everything before taking it on as yours or allowing it into your consciousness. Accept that you can't fix all the problems you want to see fixed, and you can't "right" all the "wrongs" you see in the world. Also accept that it's possible for other people to take responsibility and create positive change and, therefore, it's not necessary for you to invest yourself in every cause or every call for responsibility that comes along. Consider choosing carefully how to focus your energy in the ways that best use your talents and gifts in the directions where you *most* want to make a difference. That way, you can make a greater difference in the areas that really matter to you and in which you truly want to invest your time, energy, and focus.

Also consider *how* you are investing yourself in a particular responsibility you've chosen to take on. Merely spending time, energy, or money on something doesn't mean that your efforts are making a difference. For example, investing money in a treadmill and then investing your energy by repeatedly thinking, "I really should be using that treadmill" accomplishes nothing toward the actual goal of exercising. Likewise, repeatedly posting the same message about a particular cause to the same group of friends on social media may not be making as much of a real difference in helping the cause as more direct and effective strategies would. So check in with yourself occasionally regarding whether your actions are truly achieving your desired results, and whether you can identify other approaches or actions that would lead even more directly to your desired results.

Stress can also be a result of overcommitting yourself. Most of us experience times when we feel we've overextended ourselves by promising too much. When you just don't have enough hours in the day or you're wearing yourself out trying to meet all your responsibilities, consider the Responsibility Inventory Technique ("Responsibility Inventory," p. 54) to sort through, clean out, and reorganize your responsibility list.

Benefits

Choosing to accept a responsibility is a conscious decision to empower yourself, to take authority over that particular area and to have control or influence over how you meet that responsibility. Taking responsibility can also create a sense of purpose and meaning because you're fulfilling worthwhile commitments and building your integrity.

When you're handling your responsibilities, things also tend to go more smoothly in your life and relationships. Meeting your commitments means you get to avoid the consequences of neglected responsibilities, such as ruining a relationship or losing your house due to nonpayment. You experience fewer worries and less stress when you know that everything is being handled. Your stress level will also be lower if you're not constantly dreading negative consequences or "surprises," playing catch-up, or trying to avert disasters due to overlooked responsibilities.

When you're taking responsibility for your reactions and for working through your own issues as they arise, your consciousness is likely to be a much more pleasant place to live. Likewise, maintaining routines for health and wellness can lead to greater physical well-being and comfort.

Handling your own responsibilities also brings a greater sense of orderliness and peace of mind. You can also enhance inner peace by choosing not to take on responsibilities that aren't yours and not to attempt to control areas that aren't yours to control.

You may also notice a difference within the people around you when you consistently meet your commitments and they've learned that they can count on you, which can open the door to more rewarding experiences within your relationships.

The Process

The two techniques presented in this section can help you use responsibility to your advantage ("Taking Responsibility," p. 53) and reduce stress from "responsibility overwhelm" ("Responsibility Inventory," p. 54).

Taking Responsibility

You can use the following steps to assess a particular responsibility (perhaps a new one you're considering, one that's caused a problem because you've neglected it, one you'd like to discontinue, or each of your responsibilities in your "Responsibility Inventory," p. 54). The steps involved depend on whether you're deciding to accept or to discontinue the particular responsibility.

For each responsibility you agree to accept or continue:

1. Decide to take charge of it.
2. Set an intention to continue handling it until the responsibility ends ("Chapter 3-8: Setting Intentions," p. 71).
3. Commit to follow through on it with appropriate inner or outer actions.
4. Set an intention for exactly how you'll follow through (strategy, timing, etc.).
5. Choose additional techniques to support your success, depending on the nature of the responsibility. Examples include accepting that you're responsible for your own reactions ("Chapter 3-2: Acceptance," p. 43), making a decision to view responsibilities as a form of empowerment ("Chapter 3-14: Decision Making," p. 95), releasing any judgment against yourself as "a bad person" for neglecting responsibilities or overcommitting ("Chapter 3-5: Forgiveness," p. 61), or creating an affirmation that supports your responsibility for excellent self-care ("Chapter 3-20: Affirmations," p. 120).

For each responsibility you want to discontinue:

- Take steps to renegotiate, delegate, allow others who are already handling it to continue without you, or some other action that works for you and any others involved. (You can find some helpful tips in "Chapter 3-11: Revisiting Past Decisions," p. 85, "Chapter 3-12: Completing Unfinished Business," p. 87, and "Chapter 3-24: Mental Clean-Sweep," p. 135.)

For each responsibility you want to discontinue but must accept and continue anyway:

- Explore this as an issue to be worked through, starting with the technique in "Chapter 3-1: Working Through an Issue" (p. 38).

Responsibility Inventory

This technique can help if you're feeling overwhelmed with responsibilities or if you'd like them to be more manageable or organized. This involves a process of taking inventory of your responsibilities, then identifying how to better manage or streamline them and which you can delegate or discontinue.

1. List all the responsibilities you consider yourself to currently have, to which you've agreed explicitly or implicitly. This includes com-

Chapter 3-3: Responsibility

mitments on your mental "to do" list, chores and activities for which you have ongoing responsibility, self-care and care of others, responsibilities at work, responsibilities you've taken on as a social influencer or advice-giver, and so on. Continue until you can't think of any more. (Alternatively, you could list only your major, most time-consuming, or most challenging responsibilities.)

2. Sort each responsibility into new lists with the following category headings:

    Keep—Continue "as is."

    Keep but Reevaluate—Continue, but reevaluate how to make it easier, simplify it, streamline it, or make other improvements.

    Renegotiate—Check with whomever you promised you'd handle this responsibility (someone else or yourself) and renegotiate that agreement if the person is willing (see "Chapter 3-13: Renegotiating Outdated Agreements," p. 90).

    Delegate—Ask someone else to take over this responsibility.

    Discontinue—Drop this responsibility (because it's completed, it's no longer necessary, the agreed-upon time period has ended, or it wasn't your responsibility to begin with, etc.). Cross off or delete these from your list and consider them discontinued.

3. Shred your original list as a way of releasing the old responsibilities, keeping only the new lists of responsibilities you intend to continue. This step frees up all the mental energy previously required to hold the old responsibilities in your mind, energy that's now available to focus on your new lists.
4. For each item to reevaluate, renegotiate, or delegate, decide how you intend to accomplish that and then put that plan into action.

Examples

Here are some examples showing how you'd complete the Taking Responsibility (p. 53) and Responsibility Inventory (p. 54) techniques:

Example A

In this example, you decide to apply the Taking Responsibility technique (p. 53) to focus on your responsibility to walk the dog twice a day. The process might look something like this:

1. You decide you're going to take charge of walking the dog and make sure it gets done ongoing.
2. You set an intention to continue handling it as long as it's needed or until you decide to make other arrangements ("Chapter 3-8: Setting Intentions," p. 71).
3. You commit to follow through by making sure the dog gets walked twice a day.
4. You set an intention for exactly how you'll follow through: "I intend to walk the dog twice a day or make sure someone else does."
5. You choose to help ensure your success by making a decision to be creative and resourceful in making the most of your time, including multi-tasking by making phone calls on your walks ("Chapter 3-14: Decision Making," p. 95). You release your judgment against yourself as "a bad person" for not always walking the dog when needed ("Chapter 3-5: Forgiveness," p. 61). You then consider that in the past there have been many times when you weren't available or didn't have time to walk, so now you come up with a contingency plan to ask other family members, helpful neighbors, or professional dog walkers when you're not available.

Example B

When completing the Responsibility Inventory technique (p. 54), your inventory list might look something like the following:

- Getting to work on time
- Managing the Sullivan account
- Attending team meetings
- Checking email at least three times a day
- Grocery shopping
- Filling prescriptions
- Doing the laundry
- Maintaining the cars
- Paying the bills
- Balancing the checkbook
- Getting enough sleep
- Brushing my teeth twice a day
- Taking Friday lunch orders at work

CHAPTER 3-3: RESPONSIBILITY

- Paying my kids' allowances
- (etc.)

When you can't think of any more items, you assign each to a category, as follows:

Keep:
- Managing the Sullivan account
- Attending team meetings
- Maintaining the cars
- Balancing the checkbook

Keep but Reevaluate:
- Getting to work on time
- Checking email at least three times a day
- Grocery shopping
- Filling prescriptions
- Paying the bills
- Getting enough sleep
- Brushing my teeth twice a day

Renegotiate:
- Taking Friday lunch orders at work

Delegate:
- Doing the laundry

Discontinue:
- Paying my kids' allowances

When every item on your original list has been transferred or crossed off, you shred the original list to release it. Finally, you follow up to on the four action categories this way: you decide to use the Taking Responsibility technique (p. 53) to process each of the "Keep but Reevaluate" items; you plan to find another volunteer at work to handle the "Renegotiate" item; you'll handle the "Delegate" item by asking every family member to do their own laundry; as for the "Delegate" item, you'll inform your kids that you're discontinuing allowances because they're now all older than 18 and are responsible for their own incomes.

Chapter 3-4

Processing Emotions

Emotions are like pent-up energy which can be released through allowing yourself to express the emotions fully. Processing through emotions involves expressing whatever emotion you're feeling in each moment, keeping the emotional energy flowing outward until the emotions have run their course and subsided.

When expressing your emotions, you must do it in a safe way that does not harm yourself or others. You do not need another person with you to express yourself to—you only need to express how you feel in words. The point is expressing, not expressing *to* someone. If at any time you feel the emotion is such that you might harm yourself or others, stop and seek assistance from a health professional to facilitate you with your process.

To process through emotion, express in words what you are feeling—such as "I feel sad" or "I feel angry"—using words to give a name to the emotion and characterize what you are feeling. You can express these words inwardly, or you can express them outwardly through spoken or written words. You may find that speaking the words out loud is more effective in facilitating the flow of emotion. Begin each emotion statement with the words "I feel," and do not judge or evaluate any emotions that come up. Emotions are not right or wrong, or good or bad—they just *are*. It may help to think of emotions as energy waiting to flow. By their nature, they only tend to stick around until they are fully expressed.

Benefits

Processing emotions can eliminate emotional stress you're holding in your consciousness which can decrease your inner quality of life and color your experience of everything in your life. Carrying around anger, resentment, guilt, and depression can weigh heavily on you. Releasing them can provide great inner healing. Working through emotions provides relief as your emotional burden lifts, and it also facilitates self-validation as the aspects of yourself that are harboring those feelings get a chance to be heard.

Allowing emotion to build up within yourself by not expressing it creates not only emotional pressure but also toxicity within yourself. That toxicity can be destructive to you and also to your relationships with others. If you delay expressing those built-up emotions, you'll have a lot more of them to deal with than if you had been regularly expressing your emotions in a healthy way. Think of a tea kettle with steam building up inside—you can vent the steam a little at a time, or it can come out all at once, but it's coming out one way or another.

Sometimes emotions obscure or even "lock in" an underlying issue (such as a judgment or grudge), and processing through the emotions first allows you to then access the underlying issue so you can resolve it.

Processing emotions can also lighten your inner environment, facilitate inner peace, help you find closure by working through your feelings about the past, among many other benefits.

The Process

The basic instructions for processing emotions are simple in concept: express your emotions. You can do this by speaking or writing the words that express your emotions, such as "I feel afraid" or "I feel upset." The emotions don't need to make sense, don't need to seem justified, and don't need to have a reason. You feel the emotions you feel, and that's okay. Accept all emotions as they show up, and just keep expressing. Don't judge them or label what you feel as "bad" or "good." Don't judge yourself for feeling the emotions, and don't tell yourself you shouldn't feel that way. Let the emotions flow as you express them in a safe way, and keep expressing them until they subside completely and there is no more emotion present to express. After you're done, you may need to take further action to fully resolve an issue, since emotion often overlies deeper dynamics that need your attention. Therefore, I strongly suggest completing this Processing Emotions technique as a part of the larger process of working through an issue (see instructions in "Chapter 3-1: Working Through an Issue," p. 38, the first step of which is processing emotions).

Examples

Examples of emotion statements include:
- "I feel sad."
- "I feel angry."

- "I feel afraid that I will run out of money."
- "I feel jealous of my coworker who received a promotion."
- "I feel hurt after Patricia made those comments about me."
- "I feel anxious about giving my presentation tomorrow."

Chapter 3-5

Forgiveness

Forgiveness involves releasing judgments that you have created or that you have allowed to exist in your consciousness. A judgment is a value statement that puts down yourself, someone else, or something else—often criticizing them as falling short of some standard or ideal in your mind. One way to think of a judgment is as a label of "bad" or "wrong" that you place on yourself or on something out in the world, such as "I'm a bad daughter" or "His fashion sense is so bad" or "Society is wrong for valuing money." (Note that a judgment of "wrong" here refers to the denouncement of something rather than an inaccuracy such as a wrong math calculation or wrong phone number. A judgment involves condemning someone or something in your mind, beyond simply disagreeing with them, wanting something to change, or believing that an action is immoral.)

A judgment is like a wedge you drive between yourself and whomever you are judging. When you judge yourself, you are rejecting or separating yourself from the part of you that you're judging. When you judge someone else, you are essentially rejecting them and pushing them away, creating within your mind a wall between yourself and that person. Judgments are also mentally "heavy." They're like weights you've tied to yourself that drag you down and make life miserable within your own consciousness. A judgment you've created stays in place until you release it, sometimes remaining for years without your awareness.

A judgment includes two aspects: the value statement (the aspect you consider to be bad or wrong), and the object to which you're applying that value statement (the person or thing you're judging). For example, if you judge your cousin as too greedy, the value statement is "bad for being greedy," and the object to which you're applying the value statement is your cousin. The object of the judgment could be yourself or someone else, or almost anyone or anything: a group, institution, society, the world, the

Divine, the universe, or "everybody." However, regardless of whom or what you're judging, you can release the judgment.

A judgment is often "locked in" by emotions that you've attached to it. For example, if you judge your friend as a bad friend for forgetting your birthday, you might have a lot of anger and hurt riding on top of that judgment. Before you can release a judgment, you must process through the emotions associated with it. If you ever try to release a judgment but can't, it may be a sign of unexpressed emotions that are holding the judgment in place and that need to be expressed before the judgment will release. See instructions for expressing emotions in "Chapter 3-4: Processing Emotions" (p. 58).

It's possible for a judgment to contain positive words but still be making a criticizing value statement, such as "I'll be good and not eat that pizza" or "I'm much more worthy of love than he is." Despite using positive words, in these cases you are still assessing your (or others') value according to some standard in your mind. In the pizza example, you are placing a label on yourself as "good" if you don't eat the pizza, implying that you're "bad" if you do eat the pizza. In reality, you are *you*—you are never actually "good" or "bad." Those words are simply labels you create in your own mind, and they are not in your best interest. Their effect is to threaten yourself with punishment or with bringing yourself down, both of which are self-defeating. In the example in which you claim you are more worthy of love than someone else, you're putting the other person down in an attempt to elevate yourself. You're labelling yourself as superior to the other person—when, in fact, you are both individuals living your lives in your own ways, and any ideas of comparative worthiness of love are just labels you've created in your own mind. Again, it doesn't serve your best interest to view yourself as intrinsically superior to or inferior to another human being. When you accept yourself as you are, you don't need to judge others to feel better about yourself. Instead, celebrate yourself and others as individual souls who are living a human experience, each in his or her own way.

Forgiveness has nothing to do with who is at fault or whom you consider to blame. You can release a judgment regardless of the details of the situation.

Forgiveness does not mean forgetting the past, nor does it mean agreeing to stay in an unhealthy situation or toxic relationship. Forgiving merely means letting go of your judgment—releasing the negative label you created that puts down whomever or whatever you're judging. Once you release the judgment, any other decisions regarding the matter are completely up to you.

Releasing judgments is more about you than it is about the person or thing you're judging. You created the judgment, it has been living in your mind, and now you are choosing to release it. Releasing the judgment benefits you. Sometimes it helps to remember this fact, particularly when you are having trouble finding compassion for the object of your judgment. Forgiveness also becomes easier when you remind yourself that maybe you don't know that person's whole story—you aren't aware of everything that has happened to him in life, how he deals with things, what it's like to be him, what it's like inside his head, the inner stresses he is experiencing in any particular moment. Most of us are doing the best we can given what we have, what we know, our situations, and our state of consciousness in any given moment. However, people sometimes do things, react, or handle situations differently than what you expect or want.

Forgiveness becomes easier when you can do it from a place of kindness and compassion. Processing through all the emotion attached to your judgment creates a clear space within which you can then connect with the part of yourself who can forgive as you would like to be forgiven, who can give others the benefit of the doubt or a second chance as you would like to receive, and who can look at the other person and see their essence—acknowledge the soul that exists beneath their issues and behaviors. Remind yourself that each of us is at a different point in our own learning process. We all need space to learn—to make missteps and then to figure out how to do better next time. Choose to give yourself and others the space for their own learning process. Take every opportunity to celebrate yourself and those around you—regardless of where each person is in their own learning process—and you will likely notice that forgiveness comes more naturally to you.

Benefits

A judgment is a piece of negativity that you create and then hold within your consciousness, like a dark spot that constantly emits mental toxins such as resentment, guilt, or envy. When you release a judgment, you're releasing that dark spot—thus eliminating its negative effects and allowing that spot to fill with something more positive.

Releasing a judgment can often start a broader cascade of healing within yourself. Some of the specific results you might experience include a greater feeling of peace, acceptance of yourself and others, a more positive mental environment, and "room" in your consciousness for more enjoyable ways of thinking. You may notice improvements in your relationships with people around you as you release your judgments of them. You might also find yourself enjoying new opportunities that you never would have when your judgments were acting as walls between you and those opportunities.

Over time, you may notice a shift into a more pleasant life experience resulting from your practice of forgiveness and a non-judgmental attitude. When developing a habit of forgiveness, you may start to recognize immediately when you've created a judgment (so you can then release it), then after more practice you may start to catch yourself even before you make a judgment and you can redirect your consciousness in a more loving and accepting direction. Eventually, you may break your habit of judgmental thinking altogether.

The Process

The following process shows how you can forgive by releasing any judgment of which you've become aware:

1. Say inwardly or outwardly to yourself, "I release my judgment of (say whom or what the judgment is about) as (specify what you labelled as bad or wrong)."
2. After you've released the judgment, visualize the space it occupied within you as being filled by white light or love. You can also send light to the person or thing you were judging (see "Sending the Light," p. 19).

If you can't seem to release a particular judgment, first express your emotion about the situation involving the person or thing you've judged until there's no more emotion to express (as in "Chapter 3-4: Processing Emotions," p. 58). Then release the judgment.

Examples

The following are examples of judgment-releasing statements in the process of forgiveness:

- "I release my judgment of myself as unworthy of love."
- "I release my judgment of my boss as wrong for not giving me a raise."
- "I release my judgment of Dad as bad for being gone so much when I was a kid."
- "I release my judgment of the world as wrong for not being the way I think it should be."

Chapter 3-6
Reframing

In your day-to-day activities, the way you perceive yourself, someone else, or a situation can limit you, even without your awareness. When you encounter something—such as an external event or a thought in your head—your experience of it is shaped by the way you choose to see and interpret it, what you tell yourself about it, and the labels you put on it. You might immediately label something as "good" or "bad," "wanted" or "unwanted," "fun" or "boring," instantly creating an inner frame of reference that colors your experience of that thing. Think about how differently you might experience your first day on a new job if your frame of mind was "I intend to enjoy this new adventure" rather than "I'm probably going to dislike this company and everyone who works here." The good news is that you are in control of your frame of reference, and you can change it.

Here's an example of how your internal frame of reference can make all the difference. Consider what it would be like to view a beautiful painting while wearing glasses with green-colored lenses. Everything would look greenish to you, and you couldn't see the full range of beautiful reds, yellows and blues. You might completely miss the beauty of the painting, and you might declare the painting to be boring and ridiculous. However, if you remove your limiting glasses, you can see the range of colors, experience the painting as it actually is, and enjoy its full expression. In your day-to-day life you can change the "inner glasses" through which you view yourself and the world so you can see more clearly, in a way that works better for you. This inner shift is called reframing.

Benefits

Reframing gives you power over how you experience things in your life. Even when you can't control what happens around you, you *can* control your experience of and your inner reaction to what happens. Anything that you might tend to interpret in a self-defeating way can be transformed, creating a more self-supporting, positive, and uplifting inner experience. For example, you can use reframing to transform a failure into a win ("Look what I learned") in your mind, or to transform an obstacle into a stepping stone to whatever is next ("I can use this to move forward"). When used in a beneficial way, this technique can transform the environment inside your head into a much more pleasant place.

Reframing can entirely shift the way you relate to yourself, others, events, and situations. Since labels and judgments can create a kind of "blind spot" obscuring your view of a situation, reframing can restore your full range of "vision" of a situation—allowing you to see it more clearly for what it is, and perhaps revealing opportunities you couldn't previously see. For example, if you're busy viewing a situation as a failure, you might not spot an opportunity in its midst. The ability to shift out of a "failure" mode of thinking is the reason we have innovative products like bubble wrap, which originally failed as a textured wallpaper before it was repurposed as a packaging material.

Since this Reframing technique helps you change the way you see things, you can also use it to help see your way forward when you're feeling blocked or stuck. When you're trying to solve a problem that you just can't seem to move past, instead of using the label "unsolvable problem," you might reframe the situation as "an opportunity to get really creative" or "a great chance for collaboration with others"—or some other perspective that helps you work through the problem.

The Process

The Reframing technique involves shifting your internal frame of reference through which you are viewing something external (an event, situation, person, etc.) or something internal (a thought, feeling, or other inner dynamic). You can reframe any situation that seems challenging or that's not working for you, or that you think you'd benefit from seeing in a different light. Some telltale signs of an opportunity for reframing include judgments, self-defeating language, and frustration, or when you notice that you're fighting against a particular thought, feeling, or situation in your life. Consider how you might reframe the situation in a way that works better for you, that highlights an opportunity or lesson, that can help move you forward and upward, and that is a win-win situation for you and others involved. In other words, think of how you can remove your distorted lens of negative or limited perception and shift into a lighter, more self-supportive way of seeing.

The reframing process involves these two steps:

1. Identify something within or around you that you'd like to reframe.
2. Create a new frame through which to view the situation by removing the current frame (your current perspective and labels) so you can see the situation more clearly (neutrally). Replace the old way of viewing the situation with a new way that's more accurate, neutral, positive, or beneficial to you (and to any other people involved).

Examples

The following examples illustrate how you might use the Reframing technique to shift the way you relate to a particular aspect of your life:

Example A

Consider if you really disliked your long, boring commute to work on the train. You decide to reframe your commute time as "dream time" during which you work toward your personal dreams and goals, such as writing the book or screenplay you've always wanted to write or studying for your next career. Another idea is reframing your commute as "fun time" for surfing the internet, reading the latest bestseller, or other activities you enjoy. You could also reframe it as a chance to plan your day and catch up on messages or as quiet time when you meditate or reconnect with yourself.

Example B

Imagine a situation at work in which a new coworker keeps bugging you with questions about your group's guidelines for completing engineering reports. You view the coworker as a pest who won't leave you alone. You choose to reframe this situation in a way that works better for you. First, you shift your frame of view of your coworker to see her as a team player who's eager to learn and contribute to the group. This new view changes your attitude about the person and seems like it will make your interactions more pleasant. You also shift your view of the situation, now viewing it as an opportunity to practice your training skills. Training this coworker in group procedures will enable you to add "procedural training" to your performance report and resume. You also reframe the situation as an opportunity to improve your team process by documenting your group's guidelines, thus streamlining the group's work, reducing future interruptions with questions about guidelines, and allowing you to add "documentation experience" to your performance report and resume.

Chapter 3-7
Transforming Beliefs

Beliefs are ideas that you take as fact, whether or not they are accurate or have been verified in any way. We form some of our beliefs based on what we observe in our own experience, such as the belief that "It gets dark at night." Beliefs can also come from other people, such as from scientists telling us that "Eating vegetables helps keep us healthy." We also form beliefs by coming to our own conclusions or making assumptions, such as "My sister is trustworthy." Some beliefs show up in our consciousness without us even realizing where they came from, such as "I don't deserve a decent income" or "People don't like me."

Just because you believe something doesn't mean that it's accurate or rational, or even that it rings true for you or works well for you. In fact, some beliefs can work against you, such as the following types of beliefs:

- **Outdated beliefs**—Beliefs that you formed in the past but that no longer ring true for you, such as beliefs that you formed when you were too young to know any better. Examples include a belief that "I'm not a good learner" that you formed based on your experience in second grade, or a belief that "My opinions never matter," which you based on your parents ignoring your opinions when you were a child.
- **Irrational beliefs**—Beliefs that have no logical basis or no basis in reality, or that conflict with verifiable facts. Examples include the belief that "No one loves me," when in fact you have family members and friends who love you very much, or "If I don't get an A on this test, I'm a complete failure in life," when in fact the result of one test won't likely destroy all of your chances for success in the future—and besides, "success" and "failure" are completely subjective. Irrational beliefs are often weighted down with emotion waiting to be expressed (for more about expressing emotions, see "Chapter 3-4: Processing Emotions," p. 58).

- **Implanted beliefs**—Beliefs that were not originally your own, but that you adopted by picking them up from another person, group, the media, or another source outside yourself—perhaps without your awareness, and in some cases through no conscious intention on the part of the source. Just because a belief was implanted doesn't mean it doesn't serve you well, but because implanted beliefs were not yours to begin with, they're worth reevaluating. One example is an implanted belief that "I can never be an artist," which was based on overhearing your first grade music teacher tell your mother that you have no artistic potential. Other examples include creating a belief that you'll only be acceptable if you wear a certain brand of sunglasses, based on ads you saw depicting that idea—or creating a belief that it's okay to steal if you're doing it to help someone else, which you picked up while watching a movie depicting such activity as acceptable. A belief can also become implanted into your consciousness as a result of hearing it repeated over and over again. Repeated statements from others can be particularly tricky because they can slip past your critical thought process and lodge into your consciousness without your awareness. One example might be a belief that women must always wear makeup, which became imbedded in your consciousness after repeatedly hearing your grandma say, "You're never fully dressed without your makeup." Another example is a belief that you could never start your own business, which you formed after repeatedly hearing that successful entrepreneurs are all big risk takers (which you feel that you're not).

Beliefs can become self-fulfilling prophecies. For example, if you create the belief that "I can't trust anyone," then you probably can't—not because all people are untrustworthy, but because this belief keeps you from allowing yourself to even try to trust people. You have closed your mind to the idea of trusting people. If you create a belief that "I can't do anything right," it can become like an affirmation as you repeat it to yourself, and it may start affecting you subconsciously in a way that leads to mistakes you wouldn't otherwise make, such as by undermining your confidence.

Benefits

You may choose to transform your beliefs that you decide are inaccurate, irrational, or don't ring true for you because you feel they are holding you back, causing you to miss valuable experiences, or simply polluting your inner environment. For example, think about how your interactions with people might change if you transformed the belief that "People are basically unsocial" into "People are basically friendly," or if you transformed the belief that "I'm not good at talking to people" into "I'm learning to be a better conversationalist." Beliefs can color your perception of everyone and everything you experience in life. You give beliefs great power when you let them take root in your consciousness, so be wise about what you choose to believe. When you are mindful of your beliefs and you consciously decide which you'll hold onto, you take back your own power. Your beliefs about yourself can deny your worth and bring you down, or they can support you and lift you up—you get to decide.

The Process

Here are the steps in the process for Transforming Beliefs:

1. Identify the outdated, irrational, or other belief you've decided to change because it's not serving you well.
2. Release the belief by saying inwardly or out loud, "I release the belief that *(say the belief you want to transform)*."
3. Choose a new belief to replace the one you just released. Be sure that it rings true for you and supports you (and others, if applicable) in a positive, uplifting way.
4. Replace the old belief by saying, "I replace the old belief with the belief that *(say the new belief you are creating)*."

Examples

The following examples illustrate how to release and replace beliefs:

- "I release the belief that I'll never find work that I love, and I replace it with the belief that I can find or create a livelihood that brings me joy."
- "I release the belief that I am a loser unless everyone likes me, and I replace it with the beliefs that I have no control over other people's opinions of me, and that by being myself I'll attract the kind of friends I want to be around."
- "I release the belief that I'm a bad person if I'm not constantly doing nice things for others, and I replace it with the belief that my value is based on who I am rather than what I do."

Chapter 3-8
Setting Intentions

An intention is a kind of commitment you make within yourself to act or think in a certain way. It is a determination toward a certain action or result. Setting an intention helps you commit to and follow through on something you want to do, change, or create in your life or your consciousness. When you state that you intend to take a particular action, that action automatically gets added to your mental to-do list, and a portion of your mental energy becomes dedicated to making sure you follow through on it.

Within your consciousness, an intention dedicates more mental power for follow-through than a want, hope, or possibility. If you say, "I intend to call my friend tonight," that's a stronger commitment than saying, "I want to call my friend tonight," "I hope I can call my friend tonight," or "Maybe I'll call my friend tonight." You could say, "I will call my friend tonight," but that doesn't take into account unforeseen circumstances, such as your mother needing your help this evening, or you ending up at the hospital all evening with a broken ankle. Because you can't always control future circumstances and events, you can't say with 100% certainty that you *will* do something—so you might be making a promise to yourself that you can't keep. However, "I intend" leaves room for unforeseen circumstances that you may choose to give a higher priority, so you don't have to break an agreement with yourself if something else comes up.

When you set an intention, it creates changes within your consciousness in specific ways. An intention focuses you toward action, and it "flips the switches" in your consciousness that will help you follow through on the intended action. When you say "I intend to..." you accomplish the following:

- You place yourself in an *active role* for taking a certain action, rather than a passive role of waiting or hoping for it to happen.
- You create a *connection* between yourself and that action in your mind, which makes you more likely to complete that action.
- You *commit* to taking that action, which goes beyond simply saying you'd like to do it or you want it to happen.
- You add the intended action to your *mental to-do list,* and it now will be tracked by the part of you who monitors which to-do items have been completed and which have not—again, helping you follow through on your intended action.

You can set intentions to create more of what you want in your life (and less of what you don't want) in any area where you have control or influence. One excellent way to use intentions is to set an intention before beginning to process through an issue, such as "I intend to love myself unconditionally throughout this process" and "I intend to take complete responsibility for my reactions and judgments during this process." You can also set a pre-sleep intention to help you recall your dreams—such as "Tonight I intend to remember my dreams that are beneficial to remember" (for more details, see "Pre-Sleep Intentions," p. 142). You can set an intention for an external action, such as "I intend to go to the coffee shop at 7:30 tomorrow morning," or for an internal action, such as "I intend to identify my next step in this situation." You can also set an intention for an ongoing process, such as "I intend to stay present in the moment," or for a manner of doing something, such as "I intend to relate to myself as my own best friend," or for a way of thinking, such as "I intend to focus on the value in every situation." Intentions can be powerful tools for commitment and change in all areas of your life.

Keep in mind that you can only intend things regarding matters in which you have influence or control. For example, you can't intend something for someone else. "I intend for John to loan me $50" doesn't make sense because it's up to John whether he decides to loan you the money or not, and you are not in control of his decision. You also can't intend something out in the world where you don't have influence, such as "I intend for the hurricane to move away from our area." You may *want* the hurricane to go away, but you can't intend for it to go away because the hurricane is not within your control.

You also can't intend something in a situation in which you're involved but you have no control. For example, when traveling on a plane, you couldn't effectively set the intention "I intend for this plane to land safely." As a passenger, you may *hope* the plane lands safely or *want* it to land safely, but you have no control over landing the plane safely unless you're involved in flying the plane. If you were the pilot of the plane, you could intend to land the plane safely, but as a passenger you can only intend things over which you have control, such as in the intention "I intend to stay calm and breathe deeply during the landing process."

You can release or replace intentions if they become outdated, circumstances change, you change your mind, or for any other reason. However, once you set an intention, your consciousness relates to it as a commitment: the intention remains in effect in your consciousness until you cancel it (similar to the way your consciousness relates to a decision, as described in "Chapter 3-11: Revisiting Past Decisions," p. 85).

Benefits

Intention setting is an extremely effective tool of self-empowerment—bolstering your own power to act, change, and create what you want in your life. Intentions place you in charge of your own life—enabling you to direct your inner life and the way you interact with the world around you.

When you set an intention, you prompt yourself to act and you motivate yourself to follow through on that action. In the moment that you set an intention, you place yourself in an active role, connect yourself to that action, and begin tracking that action on your mental to-do list. When you set an intention, your mental energy instantly starts moving toward that action, generating a momentum that carries you forward through the completion of the action.

An intention also directs your consciousness to "focus on this action or direction" rather than on some other action or in some other direction. Therefore, you can use intentions to redirect yourself away from self-defeating habits or ways of thinking. For example, you might set an intention such as "I intend to pack a delicious, healthy lunch for work every day" to avoid being tempted by unhealthy food in the cafeteria. You might set an intention of "I intend to notice every time I talk to myself in a self-defeating way," so that you can then replace each instance with positive self-talk.

Once you start working with intentions, you may discover that you're more powerful than you realized, and you're able to create situations and experiences that bring joy beyond what you've ever imagined. Don't be afraid to think big and think happy.

The Process

The following steps show how to set an intention:

1. Decide what intention you would like to set. Remember, you can only set an intention in an area of your life that is within your control.
2. State your intention within yourself or aloud by saying, "I intend (*say what you intend*)." This intention will remain as a form of commitment in your consciousness until you cancel or release it.

Examples

Here are some examples of setting an intention:

- "I intend to talk to Ian today about our project schedule."
- "I intend to travel to the west coast of Australia someday."
- "I intend to celebrate the uniqueness of each person I meet."
- "I intend to be mindful of the thoughts that enter my mind and choose wisely the ones I allow to linger."
- "I intend to notice judgments I make about myself and others, and release them immediately." (See more about releasing judgments in "Chapter 3-5: Forgiveness," p. 61.)

Chapter 3-9
Transforming Negative Self-Talk

Self-talk is the way you relate to yourself within your own mind, the inner conversation you have with yourself as you go about your daily life. Negative self-talk—relating to yourself in a negative or self-defeating way—can include self-judgments, self-defeating beliefs, or any other dynamics in your consciousness that put yourself down instead of lift yourself up. Examples include telling yourself "I can never do anything right," "I'm such a loser," "I'm not as likable as that person is," or "I don't deserve to be happy."

You are the only one in control of how you interact with yourself in your head. You get to choose in every moment whether to build yourself up or tear yourself down, whether your consciousness is a pleasant or unpleasant place to be, whether you live in a toxic or healthy inner environment.

The goal of transforming negative self-talk is to consciously shift your inner narrative into one of unconditional love. One way to think about this is speaking to yourself the same way you would speak to someone whom you love dearly, a precious child, or someone you admire—or in the way that someone who loves you would speak to you. Be kind, gentle, and encouraging with yourself. Instead of punishing yourself, be patient and remember that you're doing the best you can with what you have and what you know, and you are still in a learning process (as we all are, for as long as we're alive). For inspiration, you can think of someone who is a role model of unconditional love—perhaps a family member, friend, celebrity, historical figure, or someone else who always loves, encourages, and uplifts—and imagine what that person would say to you in any moment as you are going about your life.

Sometimes positive self-talk can feel less than genuine when you're not really "feeling it"—and that's okay. Do it anyway. Keep it up, and it will likely start to come more easily and naturally. After practicing it enough, it eventually will become second nature to you—the genuine way you interact with yourself.

Benefits

Using positive self-talk is one of the most effective ways to immediately and directly improve the quality of your day-to-day experience. If negative self-talk creates a toxic environment within your consciousness that can limit you and darken your experience of everything in your life, then shifting to positive self-talk can cleanse, lighten, and open your "inner doors" to new possibilities.

Transforming your inner dialogue from self-defeating to self-encouraging can improve self-esteem and confidence, as well as remove inner blocks to personal growth. It can also transform your interactions with the world in all areas of your life. Consider how different life might be if you replaced an inner statement of "Life is boring and difficult" with "I find the humor and joy in every situation."

One of the most profound benefits of positive self-talk is that your love for yourself becomes contagious and you begin to radiate it to others around you. The kindness and gentleness with which you treat yourself begins to extend to others around you as it becomes second nature. When you are filled with love and goodwill, it can't help but spill out to others around you.

The Process

Here are the steps for Transforming Negative Self-Talk:

1. Set an intention to engage in positive self-talk ongoing, and set another intention to transform any negative self-talk you hear within yourself to positive self-talk. You could even set an intention for a "bell to go off" in your mind when any negative self-talk occurs. (Read more about setting intentions in "Chapter 3-8: Setting Intentions," p. 71.)
2. Pay attention to your inner narrative as you go about your daily life. When you notice negative self-talk, stop your inner dialogue and pause for a moment. Release what you just said to yourself, without judging it.

CHAPTER 3-9: TRANSFORMING NEGATIVE SELF-TALK

3. Replace the negative statement with a positive one. Consider what would be a more gentle, supportive, uplifting, and encouraging thing to say to yourself. Be kind, gentle, and patient—the way you would talk to someone you love dearly, a precious child, or someone you admire—or the way someone who loves you unconditionally would speak to you.
4. Repeat Step 2 and Step 3 ongoing to transform your inner dialogue.

Examples

The following examples illustrate how to go about Transforming Negative Self-Talk:

Example A

You catch yourself saying to yourself, "I can never do anything right." You pause and release that statement by saying inwardly, "I release the statement that I can never do anything right," and then you replace it immediately with something like "I intend to learn from every situation," "I'm using every opportunity to do better next time," or "I'm doing the best I know how to do, and I intend to learn and improve."

Example B

You notice a well-dressed person and think, "If only I could be like that person, then people would like me so much more." You catch yourself in this negative self-talk, pause, and release that statement. Then you immediately replace it with "I celebrate my own uniqueness and all that I have to offer the world," "I accept myself for who I am, regardless of what I'm wearing," or "I intend to look beyond appearances to see the value in the person, including the value in myself."

Chapter 3-10
Exploring Projections

A projection can be described as a mental dynamic wherein you subconsciously deny something about yourself—such as a particular characteristic or tendency—and instead you attribute it to someone else. Another way to describe a projection is when you recognize an aspect of yourself in someone else, at the same time denying that aspect within yourself. A projection is a way to avoid accepting and taking responsibility for something that you judge or reject about yourself.

The classic version of a projection is a negative projection, in which you project your judgment of yourself onto someone else. You judge someone else as having an undesirable aspect, and at the same time deny that same undesirable aspect of yourself. Examples include:

- Someone who is often dishonest accusing others of being dishonest.
- Someone who judges his own body as less than perfect judging others bodies as less than perfect.
- A person who is very stingy with her money judging others as stingy.

Sometimes a projection takes the form of blaming someone else, such as:

- Someone who dislikes another person claiming that the *actual* problem is that the other person doesn't like *him*.
- Someone who often picks arguments blaming her partner for always starting arguments.

Through the process of a projection, you're maintaining a false self-image by denying in yourself the very characteristic you are projecting onto someone else as a defense mechanism. By projecting your own characteristic onto another person, you avoid experiencing your own self-judgment, and you avoid taking responsibility for your own characteristic and dealing with any of its ramifications (such as self-judgment). So, unfortunately, your judgment of yourself gets perpetuated, rather than you getting an opportunity to recognize it and release it—and your self-judgment continues to poison your consciousness.

Projections often occur completely subconsciously, so you may be unaware that you're projecting your judgment onto someone else. However, one clue is if you have a strong, immediate judgmental reaction to a person or event. When that happens, the strong reaction may point to an underlying judgment of something within yourself. Practicing mindfulness can also help you recognize subconscious projections, as can techniques that bring subconscious dynamics into your awareness, such as free-form writing ("Chapter 3-22: Free-Form Writing," p. 127) and dream interpretation ("Chapter 3-26: Dream Interpretation," p. 144).

What's great about projections is that once you become aware of them, you can see them for what they are and work through the underlying dynamics. Because a projection often stems from your *lack of awareness* of your own inner dynamics such as self-judgments and negative patterns, gaining awareness of a projection means that it can no longer rule over you without your knowledge.

Negative and Positive Projections

Just as you might project your own undesired characteristic onto someone else, it's also possible to project your own desired characteristic onto someone else—which is called a positive projection. In both positive and negative projections, you are denying a particular characteristic in yourself. A positive projection involves externalizing a characteristic you view as positive—denying that you also have that characteristic, or the potential for it. Examples of positive projections include claiming that you could never be a good leader like a certain leader you admire, or telling yourself you could never be as likable as your older sister. Another way to describe a positive projection is when an aspect of yourself "resonates" with that same quality in another person, but you deny that aspect or potential within yourself. For example, the part of you with the potential to inspire others through public speaking "resonates" when you see your favorite inspirational speaker on TV, but you deny your own potential to be an inspirational speaker by telling yourself, "I could never be an inspiration to others."

The Object of a Projection

The mechanism of a projection involves not only personal denial of your own characteristic, but also an external target onto which to project it.

That external target can be any external entity—a person, group, society, people, the world, or just about anything within your experience. For example, a projection onto society might take the form of a corrupt government official projecting his judgment of his own corruptness by claiming that we live in a corrupt society. In a projection targeted onto the world, a vengeful person may see the world as a vengeful place.

A projection is all about *you*—it's completely *within you*—and really has nothing to do with the external target, except that the target happened to trigger your subconscious recognition of something within yourself.

Dissolving Projections

First, realize that a projection is not a "bad" thing. It's just a dynamic that your subconscious mind has created within your consciousness. More than anything, it's a pointer to an area within yourself where you don't feel at peace, an area that needs your attention.

You can dissolve a projection by accepting and taking responsibility for the aspect of yourself you are denying. Recognizing a projection removes its subconscious control over you. Awareness of a projection deflates its power, like a pin bursting a balloon and letting all the air out. Once you realize that you're projecting your own issue onto someone else, take responsibility for that issue by accepting that it is *your* issue, and then you can resolve that issue within yourself. The person onto whom you're projecting the issue may or may not also have that same issue, but his issue is not yours to resolve. You can only resolve your own issues.

Benefits

A projection indicates a particular area within your consciousness that needs attention. Projections often point to underlying dynamics that perpetuate negativity within yourself, such as self-judgments and limiting beliefs—dynamics of which you might not otherwise become aware. Each projection that you identify offers you the gift of self-awareness, as well as a golden opportunity to work through related issues and release underlying dynamics that have been holding you back or bringing you down.

Each time you project your own judgment of yourself onto someone else, you may also be reinforcing that judgment of yourself. Therefore, working through those projections allows you to release your self-judgments, thereby lightening the load of negativity within yourself and improving your inner environment.

Chapter 3-10: Exploring Projections

Because projections can create walls between you and others onto whom you're projecting, dissolving those projections can also improve your relationships and interactions in the world.

The Process

Important: Remember that this process is completely for your benefit. We all project onto others sometimes. Instead of judging yourself for projecting, use every projection you identify as an opportunity to transform and heal an area within you, like untying a knot that has been binding you.

The following steps outline a procedure for exploring projections and using them as opportunities for inner transformation:

1. Explore whether your perception of a person (or related behavior, event, etc.) involves a projection:

   Look for a negative projection: Ask yourself whether there's anything about the person (or their behavior, etc.) that bothers you—anything you judge as bad or wrong.

   Look for a positive projection: Ask yourself if there's anything about the person (or their behavior, etc.) that inspires you, that you admire, or that you would like to emulate—but that you think you could never aspire to or hope to emulate. Ask yourself whether the person is reflecting some positive aspect or potential within yourself that you're denying.

2. Identify the projection:

   For a negative projection: Consider how the person may reflect back to you an aspect of yourself that you've labelled as wrong or bad. Look for that aspect in yourself—even if it's just a little, or just the potential to be or think that way, or perhaps something from your past.

   For a positive projection: Look within yourself and acknowledge that whatever inspires you about that person may also exist within you. Consider how you may already have that characteristic or ability, or the potential for it.

3. Acknowledge that the projection exists and accept it:

   For a negative projection: Say out loud or within yourself, "I acknowledge that I was projecting a judgment of myself onto someone else, and I accept that what I was judging in that person I am actually judging in myself."

   For a positive projection: Say out loud or within yourself, "I acknowledge that I was projecting my own positive characteristics or potential onto someone else, and I accept that what I was admiring in that person I was denying in myself."

4. Take responsibility for the aspect of yourself (or the potential for it) you were seeing in the person by saying out loud or within yourself, "I am the responsible owner of (*describe the characteristic or potential*) within myself."
5. Allow yourself to feel any emotion that comes up, and let it continue to flow (safely) until it runs its course and disperses.
6. Release your judgments of yourself—anything you label as bad or wrong. For each judgment, say inwardly or out loud, "I release my judgment of myself as (*specify what you labelled as bad or wrong*)." Let go of the judgment, and visualize love or white light replacing it. (For more on how to release judgments, see "Chapter 3-5: Forgiveness," p. 61.)
7. Release any judgments of the person onto whom you were projecting. For each judgment, say inwardly or out loud, "I release the judgment of (*say whom the judgment is about*) as (*specify what you labelled as bad or wrong*)." As you release the judgment, visualize it being replaced by love or white light.
8. Take action to transform any dynamics within yourself related to this projection that are no longer working for you. For example, you might decide to transform negative beliefs or self-talk, and then set an intention for a new way of thinking. (For more about follow-up techniques, see "Chapter 3-7: Transforming Beliefs," p. 68, "Chapter 3-9: Transforming Negative Self-Talk," p. 75, "Chapter 3-8: Setting Intentions," p. 71, and other techniques in "Part III: Haven-Building Toolkit," p. 35.)

Examples

Here are some examples that illustrate the Exploring Projections technique:

Example A

The following example shows the process of exploring a negative projection that came to light:

While shopping you had a strong judgmental reaction when you overheard a salesperson trying to bully another shopper into buying a certain product. Your strong reaction tipped you off that maybe there was a negative projection involved. Upon more introspection, you realize that the behavior of the bullying salesperson may have resonated with a part of you who has bullied others or yourself (or has the potential to do so). You open your mind to the possibility that what you see in this bully also exists within you, to some degree or in some form. You ask yourself how you might be bullying others or yourself, whether there's somewhere in your life you could be less overbearing or controlling, whether you've bullied someone in the past, or whether perhaps you're afraid you have the potential to act that way in the future. You recall bullying your little brother and some of the children in school when you were a child. Next, you acknowledge your projection of bullying onto the other person by saying, "I acknowledge that I was projecting my judgment of myself onto someone else, and I accept that what I was judging in that person I am actually judging in myself." You take a few moments to experience the sadness you feel about hurting others when you bullied them in the past. Then you release your judgment of the bullying aspect of yourself by saying, "I release the judgment of myself as a bad person because I bullied others," and as you release the judgment, you visualize it being replaced with white light. You release judgments of the people you bullied by saying, "I release my judgments of the children I bullied as deserving of my bullying," letting each judgment go and visualizing white light filling its place. You follow up by setting an intention to be respectful during future interactions and to accept each person at whatever point they happens to be in their own personal growth process.

Example B

The following example shows the process of exploring a positive projection that surfaced when visiting your grandmother:

While spending time at your grandmother's house, you found yourself admiring how very loving and caring she is with everyone around her, and you think, "I wish I were like that—I could never be that kind to people."

Part III: Haven-Building Toolkit

Your comparison of yourself with someone else brings to you the possibility of a positive projection. Looking into this further, you consider that perhaps the loving and caring you observe in your grandmother also exists within you to some degree or in some form—and you then realize that the part of you that resonates so strongly with your grandmother's kindness is the part of you that's actually capable of great kindness. You decide to step fully into that part of yourself and own it. You accept the idea that you, too, have the potential to show such love and kindness to others. You allow yourself to feel the emotions that come up—including the sadness of underestimating yourself and joy upon realizing that you *do* have great kindness within you. Next, you acknowledge your projection onto your grandmother by saying, "I acknowledge that I was projecting my own positive characteristic onto my grandmother, and I accept that I was judging myself as inferior to her." You then release your judgment of yourself by saying, "I release my judgment of myself as incapable of great kindness." As you let go of the judgment, you visualize it being replaced with white light. You then follow up by setting an intention to practice more kindness in your interactions with others.

Chapter 3-11
Revisiting Past Decisions

Since childhood you've been making decisions about yourself, your place in the world, and how you interact with others. At age three you might have decided that you were going to be independent and do everything yourself with no help from others. At age eight perhaps you decided that because you felt different from other kids, you would stop trying to fit in with them. At age 14 you may have decided that being pretty or handsome was more important than anything else, and that you would make that your highest priority. At age 16 you may have decided that you wanted to be nothing like your parents and you set out to do everything as differently from them as possible. You may not realize that these decisions can stay "locked into" your consciousness until you consciously release or replace them. Decisions you've made in the past that are now outdated can limit you, the way you think about yourself, and the way you relate to the world—even if you're unaware that those decisions are still in effect.

Identifying outdated decisions can be challenging, especially if you don't remember making them. You can find clues about them by considering what in your consciousness isn't working for you. For example, if you suddenly realize you're not willing to spend an hour every day on your beauty routine, you might delve into why you started spending that much time in the first place, which may prompt you to remember your old decision to make beauty your top priority—and now provide you an opportunity to revisit that decision and release it.

Benefits

Because outdated decisions can limit you in ways you no longer desire, releasing them offers freedom and a fresh start. Starting with a clean slate, you are no longer held to old rules or constraints of the past. You might choose to replace the old decision with a new one that propels you forward into the kind of life experience you desire, or you might simply enjoy your newfound freedom from your limiting decision.

Outdated decisions may be influencing your priorities, current decisions, and actions even without your awareness. Identifying and releasing decisions that no longer work for you can instantly improve your life, enabling you to live and think in a less affected way and live more freely and authentically.

The Process

Revisiting Past Decisions involves the following steps:

1. Identify a past decision that is now outdated—that no longer serves you well or enhances your quality of life.
2. Release the decision by saying to yourself or outwardly, "I release the decision to (*say what the decision was*)." Alternatively, you can write the decision on a small piece of paper and then tear it up to symbolically release it.
3. (Optional) Make a new decision to replace the one you just released. Consider its potential effects or limitations in the future, and be sure that it's a decision that's wise to make. Alternatively, you can replace the old decision with an intention or other dynamic.

Examples

The following are examples of releasing outdated decisions:
- "I release the decision to be completely independent and never accept help from anyone."
- "I release the decision to make my top priority trying to control what other people think of my appearance."
- "I release the decision to never love anyone else after my most recent relationship ended."

The following are examples of releasing and replacing outdated decisions:
- "I release the decision to hide my intelligence so others don't judge me, and I replace it with a decision to apply my abilities to benefit myself and others."
- "I release the decision to do whatever I have to in order to fit in with others, and I replace it with a decision to foster a few great friendships with people who accept and appreciate me as I am."
- "I release the decision to not be anything like my parents, and I replace it with a decision to accept them just as they are, and I set an intention to learn what I can from my experience with them."

Chapter 3-12
Completing Unfinished Business

Unfinished business from the past can leave you with a sense that you've left something incomplete, unsaid, or otherwise unfinished. Perhaps you didn't get to say goodbye to your grandmother before she died or you never thanked your favorite teacher for changing your life. Maybe you left a promise unfulfilled, you neglected to say you're sorry for a wrong you committed, or you never got around to doing something you promised yourself you'd do. Unfinished business creates a sort of "pregnant pause" within your consciousness, wherein a part of you keeps expecting something more to happen in order to complete the action that was left incomplete. These incompletions can nag at you constantly from the back of your mind—often subconsciously—expending valuable mental energy until you take steps to complete or release them.

If you have unfinished business that involved another person, it's possible to reach closure regardless of whether you interact with that person now. In these cases, taking action within yourself is often sufficient—such as expressing your feelings, saying what was left unsaid, releasing judgments and outdated promises, and then releasing the matter. If you made a promise or had an agreement with someone, and it's not too late, you can fulfill that promise or agreement, and give the other person the opportunity to fulfill her part of it. Alternatively, you can renegotiate the agreement and change the terms, or even cancel it if you both agree to do so (see more in "Chapter 3-13: Renegotiating Outdated Agreements," p. 90).

Unfinished business comes in many forms that can exist all around you in your life: items on your to-do list, projects you began and never finished, things around the house that need to be repaired, and anything you've ever told yourself you'd do. Even the dishes in the sink, unpaid bills, and baskets of unwashed laundry are incompletions. As long as they remain undone, they are sapping bits of your mental energy. When you complete them, the mental energy previously devoted to tracking them suddenly becomes available again.

Benefits

Think about the satisfaction and sense of accomplishment you feel each time you complete and cross an item off of your to-do list. Each completion lifts a weight from your consciousness and frees up the mental energy that was previously required to maintain that item on your mental to-do list. To get an idea of how much energy is involved, starting listing in your mind all the major projects on your to-do list, and everything else you've promised yourself you'd do, but haven't—and notice how tired you begin to feel just thinking about all of them. That mental list can be a subconscious drain on your energy all the time, as can the dread, guilt, overwhelm, or other feelings about those things hanging over your head.

Completing unfinished business can also enable closure, healing, and peace within you. The results of reaching closure can range from the satisfaction of returning the tool you borrowed from your neighbor last year, to the profound healing brought about by finally saying what was left unsaid to your estranged father.

The Process

The method for completing unfinished business depends on the nature of the unfinished business and the steps you feel are necessary to reach closure. In some cases you can simply complete the action you originally promised, such as sending your cousin the photos you said you'd send him, or repaying the money a friend loaned you. In other cases you can express things that were left unsaid, or write a shred letter (see "Chapter 3-23: Writing a Shred Letter," p. 132) to apologize for a broken promise to someone who is no longer living. Another option is to inwardly visualize expressing to the other person everything you still have to say to them. In some circumstances, you may feel you need to contact someone from your past, such as to renegotiate an old agreement, or to thank or apologize to someone. Some incompletions result from a situation in which someone else hasn't fulfilled an agreement with you. In that case, decide what you need in order to reach closure—such as reminding her of the agreement and giving her an opportunity to fulfill it or renegotiate it with you, or choosing to drop the matter and release any judgments of the other person.

CHAPTER 3-12: COMPLETING UNFINISHED BUSINESS

The basic steps involved in completing unfinished business are:

1. Identify what feels incomplete from your past.
2. Identify what you need in order to reach closure and feel complete in that matter. Decide exactly what actions you will take.
3. Take the actions you chose in the previous step.
4. Release any judgments you've made of yourself or others, such as judging yourself as a bad for leaving this matter incomplete (see "Chapter 3-5: Forgiveness," p. 61).

Examples

The following examples show how you might use this Completing Unfinished Business technique to reach closure on matters from the past:

Example A

A junior high science teacher inspired your early interest in the sciences, which you followed into your career as an engineer. When you discover that your teacher is still teaching at that school, you realize that you never thanked her. You decide to visit her, tell her your story, and thank her for the difference she made in your life—and you follow through on that plan.

Example B

From the time you were a small child, your mother promised that someday she would take you to visit your family's ancestral homeland. However, she died before she could fulfill this promise. You feel sad that you never got to travel there together. You also feel angry that your mother didn't take you there sooner—that she waited too long. To complete this unfinished business, you might decide to write your mother a shred letter (see "Chapter 3-23: Writing a Shred Letter," p. 132) or visualize a conversation with her in which you express your thoughts and feelings. Afterward, you release any judgments against her regarding the past, and you release your judgment against yourself for judging her (see "Chapter 3-5: Forgiveness," p. 61). To help bring closure, you might also decide to visit your ancestral home on your own if you feel that's something you'd still like to do, and find a way to honor the memory of your mother while you're there.

Chapter 3-13

Renegotiating Outdated Agreements

We all are constantly making agreements with others and with ourselves. Promises, plans, contracts, and vows are all specific types of agreements you make with someone else or with yourself. Wedding vows and rental contracts are both significant, official agreements. Examples of less official agreements include promising to keep a secret, agreeing to host your family for holiday dinner, or promising to help your sister move to a new home. When something changes and you can no longer follow through on an agreement, or it no longer works for you, you can ask the other people involved whether they're willing to renegotiate. They don't have to agree to renegotiate—but if they do agree, you can then update the agreement so it works for all involved, or you could all agree to cancel it.

Another category of agreements is agreements you make agreements with yourself, such as promising yourself you'll stick to your diet plan this week, telling yourself you'll visit Japan someday, or vowing that you'll learn to play the piano. When you make these kinds of statements to yourself (or to other people, about yourself), your consciousness treats them as if they are contracts with yourself. They stay on your mental to-do list—consciously or subconsciously—until you cancel them or renegotiate them with yourself. If you're feeling overwhelmed, unfocused, or scattered in your life, it could be because you've made too many agreements with yourself, or maybe you're bogged down with outdated agreements or conflicting commitments you've made with yourself.

Consider how many agreements you've made with yourself that are still active in your consciousness right now. First, consider how many agreements you've made with yourself already today. They might include a plan

CHAPTER 3-13: RENEGOTIATING OUTDATED AGREEMENTS

to go to the dry cleaners, meet a friend for lunch, and balance your checkbook. Next, consider agreements you made in the last few days, such as your intention to go to bed earlier and your plan to take a workshop this month. Add to those your ongoing agreements with yourself like arriving at work on time, eating five servings of vegetables and exercising 30 minutes every weekday. Now, add to those all the outstanding agreements you've ever made in your life, including all the things you've committed to doing but haven't yet, everything you've thought about doing "someday," and all the projects you've ever started but haven't finished. Remember to include your commitments to others, such as to "love and cherish" your spouse, to pay your rent and other bills, and all of those Terms and Conditions you've agreed to on websites you've visited. Even if you only counted every agreement you've ever made that still requires action from you, that number would probably be in the hundreds, if not in the thousands. That is a huge number of uncompleted to-do list items. Consider that each uncompleted item occupies a tiny fraction of your mental energy, which in those high numbers could be sapping quite a significant amount of your energy (as described in "Chapter 3-12: Completing Unfinished Business," p. 87).

Conflicting agreements can also sap a lot of mental energy, especially if you repeatedly run up against them (perhaps because you don't recognize them as conflicting) or spend a lot of effort trying to reconcile them within yourself. An example of a conflicting agreement with yourself might be a situation in which you're staying up all night to finish tomorrow's report perfectly to impress your boss, but you also promised yourself you'd sleep plenty tonight because you feel like you're getting ill. You've made an agreement with your boss to complete the report by tomorrow, an agreement with yourself to complete the report perfectly, and an agreement with yourself to sleep tonight so you don't become ill. So, you might consider how to renegotiate some or all of these agreements in support of yourself, perhaps replacing your goal of absolute perfection (which would take many hours longer) with a goal of preparing a good report that gets the job done to your boss's satisfaction, even if it doesn't meet your own lofty idea of perfection. Because you can now finish the report in a shorter time, you can still keep the other two agreements: finishing by tomorrow and getting some sleep.

Benefits

Agreements can really pile up and clutter your consciousness. Each agreement you make requires ongoing mental energy to hold that agreement in your consciousness until you've fulfilled, renegotiated, or cancelled it. By the time you become an adult, you may have thousands of agreements floating around in your head, many of which you have forgotten about—such as telling your grandmother when you were 13 that you'd help her finish the family scrapbook, or promising yourself when you were 17 that you're going to learn kick-boxing. These agreements can weigh on you without your awareness, sapping your energy and cluttering your consciousness while you're trying to focus on other things. So, becoming mindful of and renegotiating agreements can free up that mental energy, as well as the energy being expended on the associated stress, guilt, and expectations.

Also, each agreement that you do not fulfill eats away at your personal integrity—the part of that who keeps tabs on your promises and makes sure you fulfill them—thereby eroding your trust in yourself to fulfill commitments. You may begin to not trust yourself to follow through on any agreements you make. Rebuilding trust in yourself can be a long process, just as is rebuilding trust in other people who have let you down. So, renegotiating outdated agreements can maintain healthy personal integrity and self trust, provide more mental energy, and clear the way for you to focus on what's important to you in your life right now.

Another important benefit of renegotiating agreements is that it helps you honor agreements you've made with others, which can contribute to relationships built on mutual trust. Honoring agreements with friends and family helps maintain healthy relationships, honoring your agreements at work can perpetuate job security and career success, and honoring your financial agreements (such as paying bills) enables you to maintain the type of lifestyle you desire.

The Process

To use the technique for Renegotiating Outdated Agreements, identify an agreement with yourself or someone else that is no longer working for you—one that you would like to renegotiate. Then follow one of the two processes below, depending on whether you made the agreement with yourself or with someone else.

For each outdated agreement with yourself:

1. Decide how you would like to change the agreement you made with yourself. You might choose to redefine, postpone, or cancel it. Alternatively, you might decide to redefine it as something other than an agreement—for example, as a possibility or an idea.

Chapter 3-13: Renegotiating Outdated Agreements

2. Release yourself from the old agreement by saying inwardly or out loud, "I release myself from the agreement to (*state the old agreement*)."
3. (Optional) Replace the agreement with a new agreement by saying to yourself or out loud, "I agree to (*state the new agreement*)." If you decided to redefine it as something other than an agreement, such as a possibility or idea, make a note to revisit at some point.

For each outdated agreement with someone else:

1. Determine how you would like to renegotiate the agreement you made with the other person. Clarify within yourself the updated terms that would work well for you, or whether you want to cancel the agreement or replace it with a new one.
2. If you feel clear to do so, ask the person if she would be willing to renegotiate the agreement. If appropriate, let her know what has changed for you and why you would like to renegotiate. Note that you cannot force someone to renegotiate. If you made a commitment, it remains a commitment until both parties agree to change or cancel it.
3. If the person agrees to renegotiate, do so until you arrive at an updated agreement that works for both of you (or until you both agree to cancel it).

Examples

Here are some examples of applying the Renegotiating Outdated Agreements technique:

Example A

Consider a situation in which you're feeling overwhelmed due to an overabundance of real-life commitments. You realize you've stretched yourself too far by promising too many things to too many people. You might decide to ask others whether they are willing to renegotiate their agreements with you, such as postponing until you have more time or agreeing to get help from someone else instead. You might also decide to set an intention to think carefully before making future commitments (see "Chapter 3-8: Setting Intentions," p. 71).

Example B

Imagine a situation in which you promised to help a friend move into a new house. However, in the meantime, your father developed a health issue and you've promised your parents you'll stay with them that day instead of helping your friend move. In this case, you might choose to ask your friend if you can renegotiate your commitment with her—perhaps help her unpack boxes after she has moved, or maybe even help her with the cost of hiring a moving company. Another alternative would be renegotiating your agreement with your parents, perhaps by asking them if it would be okay if one of your sisters spends that day with them instead.

Chapter 3-14
Decision Making

You make decisions all day long, every day: what to do next, how to do it, and when to work, rest, eat, exercise. Even when you're engaged in an activity, you're deciding in each moment to continue it, until you decide to stop doing it. Sometimes you make decisions that you realize will have significant consequences, such as which college to attend, whether to change jobs, which people to choose as friends, and which paths to take in your life. The consequences of a single decision can range from whether you'll enjoy lunch today to what course the whole rest of your life will take. Even something as innocuous as deciding to take a later plane flight could change your whole life, for example, if on that later flight you met the person who would end up being your life partner.

When you have a decision to make, information is your friend. The more information you have about the various options, the better decision you're equipped to make. Information includes facts, but it also includes other decision factors such as pros and cons, what you really want, your intuitive sense about the various options, the likely consequences of each option, and how you would deal with those consequences.

In many cases, there's no great benefit in making a decision earlier than you have to. In fact, making a decision later rather than sooner can actually provide an advantage: you may have more information later. You can't have less information later than you have now, and you could very well gain more information by decision time—such as new options you hadn't considered, a better idea of what you want, clearer intuition, additional input from other people, and so on. Also, conditions and options may change between now and decision time. For example, consider if you decided to go on a cruise to a certain tropical island, and you booked your trip for 14 months from now. Well, maybe eight months from now the cruise line goes out of business or a hurricane destroys the island. You would have benefitted by delaying your decision to book your cruise.

Here's another way that delaying a decision can work in your favor: it allows your subconscious mind time to mull your choices and gives your intuition a chance to come forward clearly. In fact, you can open the door for intuition to come forward by taking time to engage in activities that tend to trigger intuitive insights, such as by taking a break and putting your mind into neutral, going for a walk, spending time in or around water, or centering yourself spiritually through prayer or spiritual meditation.

When you're making a big decision, you may find it helpful to "lean into" one or more options beforehand—kind of like creating a preview or a practice run. For example, if you think you might want to change your career to firefighting, you might decide to lean into that idea by interviewing local firefighters to get a better idea of what the job is like. Another example if you are trying to decide whether to write a book, you might lean into the idea by writing a daily blog, talking to successful authors about their experiences, or taking a creative writing class.

Remember that information is only as credible as its source, so be wise about where your information comes from and how much weight you give each piece. Always consider the source—the person, website, group, company, or network—before allowing information to influence your decisions. In some cases, you'll need to find out more about the source by researching it in order to evaluate and validate it.

Beware of self-defeating beliefs and negative self-talk that can lead to decisions that work against your best interests. For example, you may have bought into the self-defeating belief that "since I've already eaten something unhealthy today, I might as well just eat whatever I want today and start my healthy diet tomorrow." Other examples include "All I've done is watch TV all morning, so I might as well just blow off the whole afternoon, too" and "That person walked away from me at the party last night, and so since nobody likes me, I'm not going to any more parties." (For more about transforming beliefs and negative self-talk, see "Chapter 3-7: Transforming Beliefs," p. 68, and "Chapter 3-9: Transforming Negative Self-Talk," p. 75.)

Also, keep in mind that indecision is actually a decision in and of itself. When you are being indecisive or avoiding a decision, you are *deciding not to decide*—which results in its own consequences. If the time for the decision comes and goes and you still have not decided, you've actually *decided* to do nothing. So, consider ahead of time the consequences of nondecision compared to the consequences of making the decision and following through.

Benefits

Making well-informed, mindful decisions—for which you've considered the various options, consequences, and contingencies—can lead to better decisions and outcomes with fewer problems and regrettable surprises down the road. Completing a decision that you feel good about can immediately reduce your stress level, bring peace of mind, and reduce second-guessing yourself. When you make a decision to take a certain action, the decision promptly directs your energy in that direction and rallies your inner resources to follow through. Great decisions can also end up taking you down rewarding life paths and through experiences that bring you joy, meaning, and a sense of purpose.

The Process

The following Decision Making technique collects information upfront and allows the maximum amount of time to gain clarity about the decision:

1. Gather information—including facts, your best educated guesses, your intuitive sense, wisdom from others you trust, and anything else to support a good decision. This gathering phase might also include processes for getting clear within yourself—such as analyzing pros and cons, visualizing possible outcomes and your feelings about them, devising contingencies or backup plans, and creating space within which your intuition can come forward clearly. Allow plenty of time in your decision-making process for this important step, which may mean you need to start considering your options early.
2. Wait until the latest time when the decision needs to be made, unless you see more benefit in making the decision early.
3. Make your decision, based on everything in Step 1 and any new information that has come to light since. Ideally, choose a time when you're feeling calm, relaxed, and clear-headed, and you're in an environment conducive to good decision making.

Examples

Here are some examples showing how you might use the Decision Making technique:

Example A

You're trying to decide what to have for lunch. You've been craving pizza all week, but you're also trying to eat a healthier diet. You consider what it is about the experience of eating pizza that sounds good to you, and you realize that you're craving food that's fun and that you can eat with your hands. You decide to opt for a healthier kind of fun food than pizza. You end up eating a chicken wrap with yummy dipping sauce, and one of your favorite finger foods: grapes. You also decide to make a deal with yourself: if you're still craving pizza by the weekend, you'll have some then, after your week of healthy eating.

Example B

You're considering attending an expensive business seminar, but you're not sure if it would be worthwhile to you. You gather information on the seminar's content and instructors, read past reviews, talk with people who have attended in the past, consider the benefits you expect to receive—such as knowledge, skills, certification, and new business contacts. You check with your supervisor to see if your company will help cover the costs, and then consider what it would cost you within the context of your current financial situation. You explore the idea of attending the seminar by imagining the experience you'd have there and how you would apply its benefits afterward. You make a list of pros and cons of attending. The seminar has plenty of space, so you wait until just before registration closes to decide. After you've gathered all the information you can, you weigh all the facts, the cost and expected benefits, and your intuitive sense, and you decide to attend the seminar.

Chapter 3-15
Leaning into Your Strengths

You can probably come up with a short list of your strengths pretty easily—things you're good at or that you like about yourself. However, you may forget some of the things you excel at—or you may have gifts that you underestimate, take for granted, or don't value. You might also have hidden strengths you don't realize you have, or potential ones that you haven't fully developed yet. When you're aware of your strengths, you can lean into them by finding ways to incorporate them more fully into your daily life and choosing which to develop even further. Leaning into your strengths can carry you forward into rewarding areas and opportunities you might never have thought possible. Your strengths give you a chance to shine, to bring more of yourself to life.

One way to become more familiar with your strengths is by considering what you've excelled at in the past. Maybe you did well in geometry, you stood up for kids who were being bullied, or you were really good at making up stories. Another way to discover strengths is to consider pursuits that you enjoy or have enjoyed in the past. Often we often enjoy things that we do well, and whether or not you do something well, your enjoyment of it can motivate you to learn to do it well. To look for more clues from your past, you might choose to review your life—decade by decade, or even year by year—considering what kinds of activities or projects you did well at that time.

Another source of information about your strengths is other people. Consider the feedback others have given you about what you do well, or what they like or admire about you. Maybe you've heard people talk about how intelligent you are or how comfortable they feel with you, or maybe you've noticed that people really respond to your sense of humor. You can review written feedback you've received in the past, such as on report cards, in performance reviews, and even in things people wrote in your school yearbook. You can also ask people directly what they consider your strengths to be, which can provide some interesting answers. Keep in mind that other people are sharing their own perspectives, and they may not see you as you really are or the same way you see yourself. They also may not be aware of all your strengths—including hidden strengths you have yet to develop—so be sure to do a reality check within yourself regarding their feedback.

Your strengths can also show up in dreams. In your dreams, you may find yourself doing well at things you're also good at in real life—or things for which you have a natural talent or ability. For example, if you dream that you're in a meeting at work in which team members are floundering due to lack of organized thinking, and you find yourself jumping in and organizing their work process, then perhaps process design comes naturally to you and you might decide to further explore that area in real life.

Remember that a strength in one context can translate into a strength in another context. For example, if you were great at strategy when playing games as a kid, you might also excel at strategy in corporate marketing or nonprofit fundraising. If you got into trouble for always making up stories as a kid, maybe that wild imagination can pay off in a career as a novelist, video game developer, or artist. If you were great at your summer job as a tour guide in your hometown, that strength of engaging people's interest may come in handy elsewhere in your life, such as in teaching, writing books about history, or managing community outreach for a museum.

Benefits

Your strengths are part of what makes you unique. There may be no one else in the world who has the exact set of strengths you have. Your strengths represent potential ways you can provide value in the world and ways you can experience the rewards of providing that value—including the satisfaction of doing good work and doing it well.

Understanding your strengths gives you personal power. Becoming aware of your personal strengths can help you in every area of your life as you make decisions, choose life pursuits, and foster friendships. For example, being familiar with your unique strengths can help you choose an ideal career that allows you to fully demonstrate your excellence in a way that other people greatly value. Focusing on your strong relationship skills can help you strengthen and maintain successful relationships with a partner, family, and others.

A familiarity with your strengths and gifts can also help you decide where to focus your personal development efforts. Understanding areas in which you have the potential to do well can help you decide which areas to develop further. For example, you may have a knack for engineering of which you're not yet aware and therefore aren't using in your life, but that you could develop further if you knew about it. In other examples, perhaps you're a natural public speaker but still a diamond-in-the-rough who's in need of practice, or perhaps you have within you the seed of incredible artistic talent waiting to be developed.

Many characteristics that you might initially consider as having no value—or even as negative—can be translated into strengths. For example, maybe you think you talk too much. Well, that tendency could come in handy in a job that demands a good talker, such as sales or politics. Perhaps you always tend to find flaws, criticize, and pick things apart. Those abilities could translate as strengths for a job in quality control, product testing, or other pursuit in which critical thinking is important. Maybe you're great at coming up with ideas but not following them through to completion, leading you to think of yourself as a quitter. You could put those "idea skills" to use in a job where all you do is come up with ideas, such as advertising, new product idea consulting, or product naming.

The Process

The following steps show the process for Leaning Into Your Strengths:

1. Make a list of your strengths and gifts of which you're already aware. Include talents, skills, abilities, areas of knowledge and expertise, and character strengths such as boldness or sensitivity. Also include interpersonal strengths, such as encouraging or motivating others, seeing both sides of an argument, empathy, patience, good listening skills, unconditional acceptance of others, or explaining complicated things in a way that people can easily understand.
2. Review your past for clues about more strengths you've forgotten or undervalued, or tendencies that could become strengths if you developed them. Write everything you can think of that you were good at, whether or not it seems valuable to you now.
3. Ask others whose feedback you value what they consider to be your strengths. Write what they tell you without interrupting them, and then thank them for their feedback. Review their lists of strengths, and then add to your own list the ones that resonate with you.
4. After each strength you've written, make notes about contexts or situations in which it would be valuable. In other words, think about how you could apply that strength in various situations, settings, jobs, disciplines, and so on.

5. Choose how to use your strengths from your list. You might choose one or two you'd like to put into use right away or perhaps to develop further. At work, perhaps you'd like to bring some of your unrecognized strengths to the attention of your supervisor and suggest ways you can incorporate them into your job or develop them further. You might decide to include certain strengths in your resume or college application. Perhaps you have an underutilized strength to which you're so drawn that you decide to explore a career based on that strength. How you use your list is completely up to you.
6. Maintain your list of strengths, adding new ones as you discover them. Review your list periodically—not only to bolster your self-esteem—but also to remind yourself of strengths you could be using more in your life or applying in new ways in your life.

Examples

The following examples show how you might use this technique for Leaning Into Your Strengths:

Example A

As part of creating your list of strengths, you carefully review each year of your childhood. You consider what you did well, what you enjoyed spending your time doing, what games you played well, and what you tended to enjoy doing when friends weren't around. One thing you remember hearing a lot from others is that you were "very bossy," and you always had your own ideas about how things should be done. At first, these seem like negative characteristics, but then you realize that they could translate into strengths. You are a natural leader. You have strong ideas, vision, and imagination. You are also great at getting others to see your vision and join in supporting it. These strengths could translate well into a number of careers, including film making, politics, or managing a company. You've always felt drawn to politics and have enjoyed participating as an active member of your community. After some consideration, you decide to lean into these newly-realized strengths by running for city council in your small town.

Example B

You create a list of strengths that includes those you remember from your past and those you're currently using in your job as a math teacher. You ask several coworkers, friends, and family who know you well to describe what they see as your strengths. Among the strengths you hear from sev-

Chapter 3-15: Leaning into Your Strengths

eral people are your resourcefulness and your ability to come up with creative solutions to problems. You hadn't realized that you excelled in those areas, and that others considered them so valuable. Those strengths resonate with you so strongly that you decide to consider a different career in which those strengths can shine. After exploring various potential careers for several months, you decide to pursue a career in mechanical engineering, which you begin by enrolling in night classes.

Chapter 3-16
Creating More of What You Want

Creating more of what you want in life means, in essence, fostering the conditions that provide more of the kinds of experiences you want and fewer of the ones you don't want. When you decide you want something in life, it's really the *experience* of that thing that you want, rather than the thing itself. Here's an extreme scenario that demonstrates this point: imagine that you decided you wanted a house next to the ocean, and so you bought one, but then you accidentally bumped your head and went into a coma. In this case, you would *have* the house, but you wouldn't be enjoying it because you wouldn't be able to *experience* it.

You can't enjoy anything in life without experiencing it. An experience consists of thoughts, feelings, physical sensations, and everything else in your consciousness—which together form the overall experience. When you decide you want something, what you're really wanting is the experience you think you'll have with it—which you anticipate will affect you in certain ways.

So, if what you desire is not the actual thing or situation, but instead the experience that you expect it to trigger within you, then here's where the real power comes in: *you have the power to create any experience within yourself at any time.* You don't have to rely on external factors to create enjoyable experiences within your consciousness.

When you start realizing that you can create your own experiences rather than believing that the external things are what create those experiences, you'll realize that you are the one with the power to create your experiences—and there are many ways to do that. For example, if you decide you want a job that you love, what you really want is the *experience* of loving your job, of enjoying your work and your relationships with

Chapter 3-16: Creating More of What You Want

coworkers. So, if you open your mind you may realize that there are many ways you could love your job and enjoy your work, including changing the ways you think about your current job and relate to your coworkers, or looking for a new job. In another example, if you decide you want a new car, what you really want is the experience that you expect to have if you get a new car—perhaps feeling happy about having given yourself a gift, enjoying other people's positive reactions, and feeling inspired by the beauty of the car. So, if what you really crave is receiving something wonderful, positive reactions from others, and inspiration from your surroundings—then there are many ways you can create those experiences without buying a new car. The lesson here is that you can ask yourself when you find yourself wanting something, "What is the *experience* I want, at the most basic level?" and then get creative about all the different ways you could create that basic experience for yourself.

Keep in mind that being creative about how to provide yourself with experiences does not mean cheating yourself out of the experience you really want. Instead, it's about determining what you really want at the most basic level—the experience level, rather than the thing, person, or situation think you want—and then exploring the different ways you can create that desired experience in your life to deliver an experience that works for you.

In some cases, a desire for something can point to an underlying issue to be resolved. In an example, maybe you saw a fantastic $500 pair of pants that you feel you absolutely must buy. You stop and consider what basic experience you're seeking, and you conclude that you want that satisfaction of feeling good about yourself when you look in the mirror, and you enjoy the looks you receive from others when wearing something interesting or different. Then you realize that spending a large amount of money on yourself also seems to confirm your value to yourself, and leads to you feel more worthwhile. Once you recognize your issue of needing to feel more valuable—of not feeling valuable enough as you are—you decide to work through that issue (see more in "Chapter 3-1: Working Through an Issue," p. 38). After you've released underlying judgments of yourself regarding your self-worth, you revisit the idea of buying these pants and notice that the "charge" has faded from that desire.

You may be thinking that what you really want is to get rid of a certain horrible situation your life. So, what's really happening in that case is that you're experiencing that situation in a way you don't like. (Of course, if the undesired situation is a harmful one, then you must use common sense, remove yourself from it and seek help, as appropriate.) Once you start considering how you can change your *experience* of that situation, you are suddenly in a more powerful position because *you* are the one who's in charge of how you experience things. *You* are in charge of your own consciousness. So, you can choose to shift the way you relate to the situation so that your experience is a more positive one. For example, if you are bored out of your mind in Economics class, you could set an intention to find interesting things about the class topics, perhaps enhancing your interest through extracurricular reading or watching economics videos on the internet. Alternatively, you could decide to play a game of figuring out how each topic could relate to you in your life at some point, how it could affect the world you live in, or find some other way to become engaged with the material. Another idea is that you could *imagine* you're interested in Economics and see if eventually it does begin to peak your interest.

You tend to get more of what you focus on, so focus on what you want. Don't fall into the trap of becoming preoccupied with what you don't want, which does the opposite of what you really want—it places that unwanted situation at the front-and-center of your mind and focuses your energy on it. Focusing on what you don't want is kind of like continually pressing the button on the car radio for the station you dislike, rather than the one you like. The more you dwell on what you don't want or what you dislike, the more energy you give it. Dwelling on negativity is like building a mansion in your mind and allowing negative thoughts to take up space there, rent-free. Your mental energy would be much better used to focus on creating experiences that you *do* want.

Benefits

Creating what you want puts you in the driver's seat in own your life. Rather than relying on others or on external circumstances, hoping they'll deliver what you want, you're taking responsibility for creating the experiences you desire. By taking responsibility for your own happiness, you shift the way you experience the world around you by changing the ways you think about it and react to it: the world does not exist to make you happy—instead, you are in charge of your own happiness. If you don't like a certain experience you're having in your life, you can change the situation—or change the way you relate to the situation in order to change your inner experience of it (read more about how to change your frame of mind in "Chapter 3-6: Reframing," p. 65).

When you find yourself wanting something in life—an object, relationship, activity, and so on—if you can understand the actual experience you are craving (excitement, entertainment, security, etc.), you may find that there are many different ways to bring yourself that essential experience.

For example, once you understand that your desire to go camping is really about experiencing peace through nature, you realize that you can also fulfill that desire a number of different ways—by camping, hiking, visiting a lake, or even visiting a park during your lunch break. If your desire to go camping is more about wanting some alone time, you could create that experience by going for a drive or to a movie by yourself.

Understanding the essential experience you seek will make it easier to find ways to fulfill that experience for yourself, often with less dependence on other people and external circumstances. Being creative with how you fulfill your desired experiences also makes it more likely that you *will* fulfill them somehow, and it may even save you time and money. For example, consider that a trip to the nearest big city may satisfy your weekend wanderlust just as well as a trip to the other side of the world—and you can do it now rather than waiting for vacation time from work. Again, distilling a "want" down into its most basic desired experience is not about denying yourself what you really want. Instead, it's about understanding yourself more deeply and providing more options from which to choose in order to create the experience you're really after.

The Process

Here are the steps in the technique for Creating More of What You Want:

1. Identify the experience you'd like to create, at the most basic level—the specific mental, emotional, physical, spiritual experience you're seeking. Keep driving down to a more basic level of experience until you reach the essential experience you're after. For example, if you want a new pair of boots, you may really be wanting to fulfill a need to feel pampered or loved, or perhaps to meet the physical need to keep your feet warm and dry.
2. Consider the various ways you can create that kind of experience within your own consciousness or out in the world (or both), then choose a way to create that experience. For example, if the essential experience you want is to feel pampered, you may be able to identify many different experiences that will fulfill that want (not all of which involve spending money).
3. Focus on the experience you want to create, and give it energy in your mind. For example, you might do this by setting an intention for what you want (see "Chapter 3-8: Setting Intentions," p. 71), creating an affirmation, or imagining in great detail how the experience will feel. The point is to focus your energy in a way that spurs your enthusiasm about the experience you want. In the exam-

ple of wanting to feel pampered, you might decide to create a collage of pictures showing various ways you would feel pampered, such as a new pair of boots, bubble bath, pedicure, cup of tea, or an indulgent coffee-table book.
4. Take at least one action step out in the world that begins the process of creating the experience you want. Then take another step, and so on, until you have created the experience you desire. It's okay if you don't know all the steps ahead of time. You can make them up as you go. If something doesn't work, try something else. In the example of wanting to feel pampered, you might plan to take a bubble bath when you get home from work, ask your spouse to pick up dinner on the way home, and schedule a pedicure for the weekend.

Examples

The following examples illustrate how you might use this technique for Creating More of What You Want:

Example A

Imagine that you are single and you decide you want to be in a relationship. When you consider the essence of the experience you're really wanting, you realize that you mostly want companionship and to feel needed by someone else. You consider the various ways you could create that experience, such as finding a new relationship partner, mentoring a child, adopting a puppy, or volunteering with a group that assists homeless people. You feel drawn to the idea of helping homeless people, and you decide to pursue that option. To focus your energy on this pursuit, you set the following intention: "I intend to serve and uplift people who are in need." You also envision the kind of experience you would like, including how many hours a week and how far you're willing to travel. You take action by visiting the websites of homeless assistance programs in your area, and you follow up by calling several of them and discussing how your involvement could best benefit people through their programs.

Example B

Consider a scenario in which you decide you're tired of being surrounded by people who tend to express negativity. You identify the specific experience you'd like to create as "feeling more support and encouragement from people around you," and then a more basic desire to "feel more positivity and encouragement within yourself." You consider various ways you could arrange this experience for yourself, such as discontinuing friendships with

Chapter 3-16: Creating More of What You Want

people who express excessive negativity, being more supportive and encouraging of friends and seeing if perhaps they begin to relate to you more positively, releasing judgments and updating your beliefs about your friends to change the way you experience them, and providing yourself with the support and encouragement you crave. You decide to first try creating your own support and encouragement rather than relying on others for it. To focus your energy on this, you create the following intention: "I intend to love and support myself unconditionally at all times." You also take further action within your own consciousness by practicing positive self-talk, self-forgiveness (see "Chapter 3-5: Forgiveness," p. 61), and deepening your spiritual experience to center yourself in that source of love that is always within you (see "Chapter 3-17: Deepening Your Spirituality," p. 110, and "Chapter 4-2: Centering," p. 165). You may also notice others becoming more supportive of you as you shift into a more fulfilled existence because you've been providing yourself with the support and encouragement you've been desiring.

Chapter 3-17
Deepening Your Spirituality

Strengthening your connection with the Divine is all about spending time attuning to that higher power in your daily life, and endeavoring within yourself to create a deeper spiritual connection. If you feel you don't have a strong connection with the Divine, the reason is most likely on your side of the relationship, since the Divine is always present and always available to you in the deepest way possible. The Divine is a constant, so if you want to change your relationship with the Divine, you must take action or make changes on your side of the relationship.

Sometimes you may get in your own way when trying to connect with the Divine. More specifically, certain dynamics within your consciousness can act as blocks that interfere with your ability to experience the Divine's presence. These dynamics that can block your experience include judgments, beliefs, intentions, past decisions, negative self-talk, and distractions. It might help to think of your connection with the Divine as being like a phone connection, where the Divine is always on the other end of the line, and all you need to do to connect at any time is pick up the phone on your end of the line. However, sometimes there can be static on your end of the line—such as "static" created by your judgment that you are not worthy of the Divine's attention. Another possibility is that perhaps you refuse to pick up the phone because of a belief or decision, such as the belief that the Divine does not support you based on the fact that you didn't receive something you prayed for. You can take steps within yourself to release or transform the dynamics that interfere with your direct experience of the Divine, as described in the process for this technique (p. 111).

Benefits

Deepening your spirituality can improve your life in significant and unexpected ways. Opening to and connecting with the Divine can lead to life experiences to which you've aspired—and beyond anything you've even imagined. Opening yourself fully to the presence of the Divine can result in healing, a greater capacity for love within yourself, profound peace, joy, a sense of well-being, a stronger center within yourself from which to relate to others, spiritual assistance, finding meaning in life, among many other benefits. The results of a deeper ongoing connection with the Divine reach far beyond feelings of inspiration and into profound transformation, enactment of your life purpose, clear inner vision, and exquisite peace.

The unique benefits you experience will depend on how you maintain and participate in your relationship with the Divine. Because the Divine is already present with you, your benefits will result from improving your side of that relationship so that you can experience the Divine more of the time and in a more direct and personal way. This means taking steps to enable an open connection with the Divine in all areas of your being—including physical, emotional, mental, and spiritual levels. Divine presence is healing, uplifting, transformative, peaceful, and fulfilling. So, the greater the connection you maintain—the more often and more deeply you touch into the Divine, and the more you integrate the Divine into your way of thinking and being—the more benefit you're likely to experience.

The Process

The following process can help you in Deepening Your Spirituality:

1. Release or transform the dynamics within you and other factors that interfere with your direct experience of the Divine, such as:

    Judgments—Such as "I'm not worthy of the Divine" or "The Divine is horrible for allowing bad things to happen" (see "Chapter 3-5: Forgiveness," p. 61).

    Beliefs—Such as "The Divine has nothing to offer me" or "I'm completely on my own in life" (see "Chapter 3-7: Transforming Beliefs," p. 68).

    Intentions—Such as an intention to connect with the Divine only on a certain day of the week, or an intention to connect with the Divine "later"—where later never comes (see "Chapter 3-8: Setting Intentions," p. 71).

    Outdated Agreements—Such as a "deal" you made in the past with the Divine, or a promise to yourself like "I'll never to speak to the Divine again if I don't get what I prayed for."

Past Decisions—Such as a decision not to be a "spiritual person," or a decision to not accept help from anyone else (see "Chapter 3-11: Revisiting Past Decisions," p. 85).

Emotions—Such as anger at the Divine or fear of the Divine (see "Chapter 3-4: Processing Emotions," p. 58).

Negative Self-Talk—Such as telling yourself "I'm just not the spiritual type" or "I'm not the kind of person that the Divine wants to be involved with" (see "Chapter 3-5: Forgiveness," p. 61, and "Chapter 3-7: Transforming Beliefs," p. 68).

Projections—Such as projecting your own judgmental or punishing tendencies onto the Divine (therefore seeing the Divine as judgmental or punishing).

Distractions—Such as allowing internal mental chatter or external noises to intrude on your conscious connection with the Divine. When you "get distracted," what's happening is you're distracting yourself. You're actually in control of whether you choose to be distracted or choose to stay focused. When a distraction intrudes, you can choose to let it go. You can strengthen this ability to focus through mindfulness or concentration exercises. Spiritual exercises can also reduce your susceptibility to distractions as you learn to shift to a level beyond them.

Consciousness-Altering Substances—Many people notice that certain substances tend to interfere with their ability to sense the presence of the Divine. To help raise your consciousness level and increase your sensitivity to the presence of the Divine, avoid things like sweets, toxins, and psychoactive substances.

2. Connect with the Divine. At the most basic level, all you need to experience a connection with the Divine is to direct your inner focus to the Divine. You can use a phrase such as "I open to the Divine" or a keyword such as the specific name you use for the Divine. But even that is not necessary, because as soon as you create the intention to connect with the Divine, you've already opened

your end of the connection, so the connection has been made (like picking up a phone on which the operator is always on the line). For more, see "3. Deepen into Soul" (p. 10) and "Centering in the Divine" (p. 165).
3. Stay connected with the Divine, such as through intention, focus, prayer, or spiritual exercises (see "Chapter 4-5: Prayer," p. 169, and "Chapter 3-18: Spiritual Exercises," p. 114). You may notice that the longer your consciousness remains in a state that is open to the Divine, the deeper your experience and more profound the effects. You can also consciously attune to the Divine as many times as you choose throughout the day, or set an intention to remain attuned to the Divine ongoing.

Examples

Here are some examples of ways you might go about Deepening Your Spirituality:

Example A

You might decide to connect with the Divine every morning as soon as you wake up. Before opening your eyes, you say inwardly, "I open to the Divine in all ways and in all areas of my being." For the next 15 minutes you inwardly repeat the words "Divine Love" and focus your awareness on the Divine's presence within you that is filling and uplifting you, and on your gratitude for that presence. Whenever a distracting thought enters your mind, you let it go. After you finish your meditation, you renew your intention to maintain your connection with the Divine throughout the day.

Example B

Imagine a scenario in which you have a strong intention to center yourself in the Divine as you go about your daily life. However, sometimes you feel like you pull away from that idea as you focus on various projects during the day. So, you get creative about ways to remind yourself to renew your connection with the Divine. You choose "Peace" as a quick keyword to redirect your focus back to the Divine. You put sticky notes saying "Peace" in key spots around your house, such as next to your bed and on your bathroom mirror. You find a wallpaper graphic for your smartphone that says "Peace" so you'll be reminded every time you look at your phone. You also create an affirmation of "I am one with the Divine," which you repeat throughout the day whenever you think of it. At bedtime, you spend "quality time" connecting with the Divine.

Chapter 3-18
Spiritual Exercises

Spiritual exercises are a particular type of active meditation during which you shift your awareness into soul and the Divine for an extended period. In other words, spiritual exercises involve the practice of experiencing the Divine directly. Rather than trying to empty your mind, the point of these exercises is to elevate your focus beyond the physical, mental, and emotional levels into soul and the Divine. A strong intention, sincere desire, and loving attitude make all the difference in this process.

You might start small by doing spiritual exercises for five minutes and then gradually increasing each day. The longer the duration, the greater the benefit to you. You can even do them more than once a day.

Spiritual exercises are an ongoing process that builds on itself. Similar to physical exercise, the effects are cumulative across sessions, so if you skip a few days you may notice that your next session is more challenging.

During spiritual exercises you'll need to be sitting or lying down with your eyes closed, but otherwise no specific position is required. Any location is fine (living room, bedroom, passenger seat of a car, train, etc.), although it's preferable that it be quiet and comfortable so you won't be disturbed by intrusions or physical discomfort.

If thoughts come into your mind during spiritual exercises, that's okay. When a thought appears, just neutrally observe it until it disappears. Don't try to keep thoughts out of your mind, and don't judge yourself when they do show up. In fact, don't judge anything during spiritual exercises. If you find yourself judging, just release the judgment. Just observe anything that shows up with love and goodwill and then allow it float out of your consciousness.

You can improve your experience and the resulting effects even more by taking certain steps before and during your process. Beforehand, release any expectation that you'll have any particular experience or results. In other words, be open to whatever your experience may be and observe whatever comes forward. Also, set an intention such as "I intend to elevate into the peace of soul" or "I intend to open to the releasing and healing that's available." If you lose focus during spiritual exercises, simply redirect your mind to the process at hand. Be gentle with yourself.

Sometimes you may not feel a benefit in the midst of spiritual exercises, meaning you may or may not feel elevated while you're engaged in the process. That's also okay. But you may notice afterward when you get up and go about your day, something is better or your inner world feels transformed somehow.

Occasionally you may experience an inner resistance to doing spiritual exercises. You may *think* often about doing them, but never really get around to sitting down and *doing* them. The idea is to just sit down and start. You could even make a deal with yourself that if you want to stop after ten minutes, you can. (Once you get that far into them, you'll often want to keep going.) It's also very helpful choose a daily time to do spiritual exercises, such as when you first wake up, before you go to sleep, or during your lunch hour. Creating a routine increases the likelihood of doing them consistently.

Benefits

Because you're shifting into soul awareness during spiritual exercises, this is a powerful way to build your inner haven to carry you through stressful times. The more time you spend focused into soul during spiritual exercises, the more established your consciousness become rooted in the strength of your true being. This deepening into soul brings all the benefits discussed in the earlier parts of this book. More specifically, some of the most remarkable benefits of spiritual exercises you may experience include:

- Deepening your awareness of self, soul, and the Divine.
- Enabling deep inner healing.
- Facilitating inner peace and dissolving stress.
- Elevating your consciousness and inner focus.
- Dissolving self-limitations and other obstacles.
- Releasing negativity that no longer serves you.
- Diffusing the emotional charge of inner disturbances.
- Fostering greater empathy and open-heartedness.
- Clarifying purpose and direction.
- Increasing open-mindedness and recognition of opportunity.
- Helping reduce pain or the sensation of it.
- Fostering well-being on all levels.

Amazing things may come forward within you during spiritual exercises: answers, solutions to problems, greater understanding, new ideas, clarity of purpose and the "big picture," opportunities, hidden talents and gifts, or an insight that changes everything. After doing spiritual exercises, you might notice a shift in perspective toward feeling more accepting, open, and loving toward yourself, others, and the world, and feeling less judgmental and limited by constrictive mental dynamics.

Doing spiritual exercises can also improve your ability to focus in day-to-day life, reducing your susceptibility to distractions. You may also notice heightened intuition as you learn to move into that quiet, higher state of mind in which you can more directly access it.

As you practice consistently over a number of days and months, you'll begin to notice more changes within yourself: maybe that you're feeling calmer or less judgmental in your daily life or that you're tending to notice the light in other people more. You may also realize you feel better in general, or you feel happier and more content.

At bedtime, the process of this spiritual focus can create an inner state that's more conducive to sleep, elevate your consciousness, and lead to a more uplifting dream experiences.

Spiritual exercises are restorative and rejuvenating, sometimes even more so than sleeping for the same length of time. They're also a great way to take a break from your mind, emotions, or the world, and you can use them to occupy yourself when you're bored or in a monotonous environment (such as on a trip or in a waiting room).

The Process

(Note: For safety reasons, don't do spiritual exercises when you are driving or operating machinery, or in any other situation where you need to stay mentally present or focused.)

To practice spiritual exercises, use the following steps:

1. Find a quiet and comfortable space and take steps to reduce the chance of distraction (tell others not to disturb you, get a blanket if you're cold, drink water or eat if you need to, empty your bladder, etc.). If it's noisy, you can dampen sounds with noise-cancelling headphones, white noise, fan noise, etc. (but not music because it can lower your focus into the mental and emotional levels).
2. Sit comfortably or lie on your back. (If you tend to fall asleep when lying down, bend one elbow 90 degrees with your hand in midair, so if you fall asleep it will fall and wake you up.)

Chapter 3-18: Spiritual Exercises

3. Close your eyes.
4. Call in the light by saying inwardly, "I ask for Divine light to fill, surround, and protect me for the highest good of all concerned." (See more in "Calling in the Light," p. 17.)
5. Begin spiritual exercises by inwardly repeating one of the names for the Divine such as "Hu" (an ancient name for God, pronounced as "hue") or "Divine God." Whatever name you choose, make sure that as you repeat it your intention is to reawaken to the highest power that exists (the ultimate force in the universe, the source of Divine peace and perfect unconditional love) by allowing it to fill all areas of your being and by shifting your awareness into soul.

   If a thought appears in your mind, observe it until it floats away. If you experience an interruption, close your eyes and resume.

   Keep going as long as you can. You'll eventually reach a point when you become aware of your physical surroundings again and feel complete with the process.

6. Write down anything valuable that came forward and you want to remember.

Chapter 3-19
Rainbow Visualization

The Rainbow Visualization technique helps you lift into a higher, more peaceful and positive state. You can use it anytime you want to shift out of stress and negativity and into a more peaceful, positive, elevated state of consciousness. The basic idea of this technique is that visualizing individual colors in order from a lower to a higher wavelength (or frequency) can help you shift from a "lower" to a "higher" state of consciousness.

Benefits

This consciousness-lifting process offers great benefits such as helping to:

- Clear your mind and elevate your perspective, so you can access higher wisdom more directly.
- Reduce negative mental residues left behind by certain situations.
- Attenuate huge or chaotic emotions, such as after an overwhelming event.
- Shift into a clearer state before you begin a process, such as an important conversation or decision.

When used at bedtime this technique can help you release the stresses of the day, help you fall asleep, and create a more positive state of consciousness that may result in more pleasant dreams. After a nightmare, this technique can help you clear out any lingering negativity and move into greater peace.

The Process

An easy way to remember the Rainbow Visualization technique is that it progresses through the sequence of colors in the visual spectrum—from

Chapter 3-19: Rainbow Visualization

the lowest frequency (red light) to the highest frequency (violet light), and then finishing with very light shades of gold, silver, white, and clear light.

1. Close your eyes, and call forward a Divine presence within you (or another name according to your personal preference). Alternatively, bring forward a feeling of love within yourself by thinking of a loved one or a favorite pet. (This step is the foundation for the whole process: make sure you complete it before continuing.)
2. Visualize that you are floating inside a huge rainbow, inside its red band of colored light. Visualize this red light filling and surrounding you for 15 to 20 seconds. Then float over to the orange part of the rainbow, and let the orange light fill and surround you for 15 to 20 seconds. Continue until you have visited all the colors in order as listed below. To visualize each color vividly, think of something beautiful in that color—red rose, orange sunset, yellow lemon, leafy green tree, and so on.

Red
Orange
Yellow
Green
Blue
Purple
Violet

3. Visualize yourself rising above the rainbow into a light shade of bright golden light that fills and surrounds you for 15 to 20 seconds. It then changes to a light shade of bright silver light and you continue floating in it another 15 to 20 seconds. Then repeat similarly for a bright white light, and then clear light.

Gold
Silver
White
Clear

To extend this process after finishing the last color (clear light), you can visualize a white light filling and surrounding you for as long as you like. If you have trouble visualizing any of the colors, you might find it helpful to look at a color wheel online for inspiration. Use your favorite search engine to search for "labelled color wheel" and then click an image to view it.

Chapter 3-20
Affirmations

Affirmations are a powerful way to establish and super-charge any change you would like to create within yourself or within your experience of life. As you begin repeating an affirmation, you're planting within your consciousness a seed for change and then nourishing it to take root there. For example, if you would like to experience more joy throughout your day, you might create the affirmation, "I am joyfully mindful of the simple pleasures in life." An affirmation's effect really deepens when you repeat it many times throughout the day, over a period of 30 days or more.

You can create an affirmation about anything involving yourself or your inner experience. You might create "I am joyfully living my best life" or "I am following the path of my highest purpose" or "I am experiencing the world with an open mind." However, you wouldn't use an affirmation to try to change someone else, influence something that isn't yours, or change something in which you're not involved. For example, instead of "Ben is being more open and honest with me," you would focus the wording of the affirmation on yourself such as, "I am creating a safe space for honest communication in my relationship with Ben."

The change reflected in your affirmation can be a completely new experience (such as learning something new), a change in a current activity (such as finding more enjoyment in your work life), a change to your outlook (embracing the simple joys in life), a change in direction (living a more purposeful life), or almost any other experience you'd like to create.

Benefits

An affirmation is a wonderful tool of personal power, a means for facilitating a change from one way of being to another that you find more desirable. It creates a clear direction in which to focus your energy and then harnesses the energy to flow in that direction.

At the same time, an affirmation actually *begins* the process of the change you want to see, engaging your consciousness with present-tense action language (such as "I am learning…" or "I am enjoying…"). This indicates to all inner aspects of you (mental, emotional, inner child, etc.) that the change is already in motion. You can further strengthen the commitment from all those aspects of yourself by energizing the affirmation (through focusing on the affirmation often, getting excited about it, and having fun with it).

Affirmations also serve as reminders that "This is my new way of being or thinking," repeatedly focusing your attention in that direction. The repetition of an affirmation creates a new pattern within your consciousness, a new mental habit that can persist. Each time you say your affirmation you internalize your desired change a little more and it becomes more believable, more real, and further established within you.

One of the most beautiful benefits of affirmations is their power for change over time. Consider how a river can gradually change the shape of its surrounding banks, carving bits here and there until it has eventually created a magnificent canyon. You might not notice a change from one day to the next as you practice your affirmation, but with persistence you may notice a tremendous change beyond what you imagined.

The Process

The following steps show how to create and work with an affirmation:

1. Write your affirmation. Here are some guidelines and tips for best results:

    Start your affirmation with the words "I am" to directly engage your consciousness.

    Focus on what you want rather than on what you don't want.

    Focus on the experience you want to create. Write the affirmation as if you're already having that desired experience, and convey how it feels to you in the moment. Use active experiential words (such as "-ing" verbs like "enjoying" or "celebrating") to engage your sense of what the experience will be like.

    Choose an affirmation that resonates with you, that gives you that "magical" feeling or really charges your energy. Include individual words that feel particularly meaningful to you or that "turn on a light" within you.

Use your intuition as you are writing it. The best affirmation for you will just "feel right," and you may sense a sudden feeling of peace or well-being when you arrive at the ideal version. Keep crafting the wording until you reach that point. (You're going to be ingraining this statement deeply into your consciousness, so it's worth taking your time here.)

2. Commit to practicing this affirmation for at least 30 days.
3. Choose regular times throughout the day to practice your affirmation (for example, when you first wake up, during your commute to work, during your breaks, while exercising, at bedtime, etc.) Each time, say your affirmation five times or more. You can also practice it whenever you think of it throughout the day.
4. Write your affirmation in places where you'll see it often. Write it on sticky notes and put them in your car, inside your closet, on your bathroom mirror—anywhere that will catch your eye. Get creative about other ways to remind yourself, such as setting up a recurring reminder on your electronic calendar or creating a visual touchstone (such as a picture of a sunset to remind you of an affirmation about enjoying nature's beauty).
5. Energize your affirmation with activities that focus on it. For example, you could journal about your affirmation, leaning into the change it represents and how that experience will feel. Imagine it, feel it, luxuriate in it, celebrate it—and describe that in words. Write about how wonderful it is and congratulate yourself for taking this positive step in support of yourself. Another example is to put your affirmation to music and turn it into a song that you sing around the house. This step is another opportunity to get creative.

Examples

Here are some examples of affirmations:
- "I am embracing the peace available in every moment."
- "I am fearlessly standing in my strength."
- "I am using every experience to learn and uplift myself."
- "I am confidently stepping forward to express who I am."

Chapter 3-20: Affirmations

- "I am staying present in every conversation as a way to honor myself and others."
- "I am opening to new opportunities for upliftment and service to others."
- "I am caring for myself exquisitely as the beloved soul that I am."
- "I am joyfully creating win-win situations with others."
- "I am leaning into my strengths and vast inner resources."
- "I am communicating clearly and listening attentively to others."
- "I am fostering honesty within myself and with others."
- "I am making the wisest and most nurturing choices in my daily self-care."
- "I am speaking my truth in a way that uplifts myself and others."
- "I am acknowledging my own Divinity as I allow the Divine to work through me."

Chapter 3-21
Meditation

Whatever preconceptions you have about meditation, set them aside. There are so many types of meditation, each with their own benefits, that you're likely to find at least one that works well for you. Some of the various types include:

- Mantra meditation (repeating a keyword or phrase).
- Spiritual meditation (experiencing the presence of the Divine).
- Mindfulness meditation (awareness of your mind, emotions, and body).
- Focused meditation (focusing on a concept, quality, or object).
- Contemplative meditation (focusing a topic to gain insight).
- Transcendental meditation (transcending the self using a mantra).
- Breath meditation (focusing on breathing in and out).
- Movement meditation (pairing mindfulness with physical activity).
- Progressive relaxation (tensing then relaxing each body part).
- Guided meditation (following an inner process guided by a narrator).

When starting meditation, remember that it's a practice, which means as you practice it more it will become easier and more natural. Even experienced meditators deal with doubt and resistance. If you start thinking you can't meditate or you've tried it and feel like it "didn't work," try it again. It's likely that you just need more practice. (If you were learning baseball and the first time you swung the bat you missed, you'd keep swinging. That's part of the process. Just keep picking up the bat.)

You can find more about spiritual meditation in "Chapter 3-18: Spiritual Exercises" (p. 114), and much more about all the meditation types on the internet and in books. When choosing a type, consider the benefits and effects you desire. Don't be limited by the type you think you "should" be doing or whether you think you can succeed with a particular type. Also, when you've chosen a type to experiment with, give it a good go: start with a few minutes and extend longer each session, and be consistent with at least daily sessions. As you continue you'll likely begin to see greater benefits. Be patient with yourself, stick with it, and keep moving through any resistance that may arise.

Benefits

The benefits of meditation depend to a great extent on the type of meditation you're doing. Examples include:

- Relieving stress.
- Dissipating destructive emotions.
- Improving focus and susceptibility to distractions.
- Enabling a calmer inner state.
- Helping reduce pain, or the sensation of it.
- Improving sleep quality, including the ability to fall asleep.
- Positively affecting physical health, including blood pressure.
- Sharpening clarity and heightening awareness.
- Enhancing intuition.

With most types of meditation, the longer and more often you meditate, the more enhanced the effects. Practicing meditation can also help you learn to navigate more easily between levels of consciousness, which gives you more flexibility and control over your inner state. For example, your ability to shift into a calm, neutral inner state in any moment can improve your ability to access intuition (which is most accessible when you're calm).

You can improve your meditation experience and the resulting effects by taking certain steps before and during your process. Before you begin, release any expectation of any particular experience or results. Also, set an intention for the quality of process, such as "I intend to be open to any beneficial effects this process can bring forward" or "I intend to relax and go with the flow during this process." If you lose focus while meditating, simply redirect your mind to the process at hand. Be gentle with yourself and release any judgments that arise.

The Process

The process may vary depending on the type of meditation you're doing, but the basic steps usually include:

1. Sit or lie comfortably in a quiet place where you won't be interrupted. If needed, take steps to any intrusions of noise (such as with white noise or fan noise).

2. Close your eyes and call in the light ("Calling in the Light," p. 17).
3. Maintain a particular focus for some length of time. (The nature of this focusing depends on the type of meditation.)

Examples

The following examples show the process you might use for a focused meditation and a breath meditation:

Example A

This example shows how to do a Meditation for Inner Peace (a focused meditation) to reduce stress and bring about greater peace within yourself. As you find yourself choosing toward peace more often, you may notice that the "non-peace" dynamics within you will begin to subside throughout your daily life.

1. Sit comfortably in a quiet place where you won't be interrupted.
2. Close your eyes and call in the light ("Calling in the Light," p. 17).
3. Visualize an intensely peaceful white light filling you and spilling out into the area surrounding you, extending out about eight feet around you. Take three deep breaths, and with each breath visualize light becoming even more peaceful.
4. For five minutes, focus on peace. If a thought enters your mind, simply observe as it floats in and then out again.
5. Afterwards, reflect on any insights that came forward about how you can create greater peace within yourself and your life.

Example B

Here's an example of a breath meditation that can help center yourself, relax the body, rest the mind, reduce stress, and release inner disturbances:

1. (With eyes open or closed) Bring your awareness to your breathing. Notice as the air flows into your lungs and then flows out again.
2. With each inhalation, visualize breathing in bright white light that fills your entire being. With each exhalation, release any negativity that no longer benefits you.
3. Continue as long as you like. If you encounter any distractions, simply bring your awareness back to your breathing.

Chapter 3-22
Free-Form Writing

Free-Form Writing is basically what it sounds like: a process of writing freely, continually expressing on paper whatever flows into your stream of consciousness. If you like, you can also focus your writing on a particular aspect of yourself or your life.

Benefits

Free-Form Writing is an especially useful tool for "clearing out the cobwebs" within your consciousness. Everything swirling around in there—random thoughts, emotions, worries, judgments, incompletions, ideas, inspirations, etc.—pours out of your consciousness and onto the paper. This clearing out process opens up more mental and emotional space for whatever's next, leaving you more peaceful and centered.

This process is also a powerful tool for reaching into deeper areas of your consciousness that aren't always easy to access. It establishes an outward flow through which your subconscious mind can reveal its secrets and bring to light issues that need further attention. Free-Form Writing can also bring forward deep wisdom, greater clarity, emotions waiting to be expressed, areas for healing, opportunities, unrealized gifts, next steps, creative ideas and solutions, and sources of inner strength you didn't know you had.

The Process

Use the following steps for Free-Form Writing:

1. Sit down with pen and plenty of sheets of paper that you can discard at the end. (Use paper rather than an electronic device, since destroying the pages at the end is a very important step.)

2. Start writing anything and everything that comes to mind. Don't worry about handwriting or spelling because you will be the only person who ever sees this. As you write, if anything shows up that you want to save (a great idea, a realization, an item for your to-do list, etc.), note it on a separate page to save. If your mind goes blank, just write "I am going to keep writing" and keep going. If you get stuck for a long time with nothing to write, you can ask yourself a question or prompt yourself with a statement such as "If I had something to say, it would be..." or "If I knew what to write, it would be...."
3. Keep writing until you feel complete and there's nothing left to be said.
4. Tear up or shred the original writing pages to indicate to your subconscious mind that you're releasing all the things you wrote about (after you've noted on a separate page anything you want to keep).
5. If any issues arose that need further attention, see "Chapter 3-1: Working Through an Issue" (p. 38).

Examples

The following examples show how Free-Form Writing might be done:

Example A

In this example of a Free-Form Writing process, a 24-year-old man named Jack writes what's present for him when he wakes up really early one morning:

"I hate waking up so early and then not being able to go back to sleep! So frustrating! What a waste of time when I could be doing something productive, or sleeping so I don't feel horrible the rest of the day. At least it's a nice, sunny morning. I can hear birds chirping, so I know I'm not the only one awake this early. I wonder what will happen when I go into work. I have a lot to get done today, but what makes it challenging is that I can't get it done by myself, but I really don't like relying on other people to help. Or worse yet, to show me how to do something. I'd rather learn on my own. But at least the people I work with are nice, they really seem to know what they're doing, and they don't mind explaining things to me. I have to remember to take those great leftovers from last night for my lunch today. Wow, that was a really great meal. The burger was just perfect. I didn't know vegetarian burgers could be so great. I want to try more things like that. I didn't feel weighed down after dinner like with a burger made with meat. If it tastes that good, why wouldn't I have it more often?

Chapter 3-22: Free-Form Writing

(He adds vegan burgers to his shopping list.) Let's see…what else? I feel like my mind is a blank right now, so I'll just keep writing whatever words come into my mind. It sure is early. My room is really messy. Maybe I'll spend a little time picking up around here before I shower. *(Adds this to his to-do list.)* I wonder if I have any orange juice left. Maybe I should stop at the store on the way home tonight. I could use some more salad stuff and potatoes, too. *(Adds items to shopping list.)* I really wish I could go back to sleep, but I'm not sleepy at all. Sooo, I'll keep writing. And writing. I'm thinking words and I'm writing. It feels like it's going to be really hot today. I wonder if it will be too hot to go running when I get home from work. I really want to get more of that in. I feel so much better when I run, and I sleep a lot better, too. Hey, I never really thought about that before, how working out really helps me sleep. Yeah, it's been almost a week since I went running, so maybe that has something to do with why I can't sleep. Maybe I should start keeping track of when I run and then how I feel for the next day or two. It seems like running puts me in a better mood the next day, too. So I could also keep track of my mood, like on a scale of 1 to 5. That might be interesting. Huh, even though I'm not feeling so great, I came up with some pretty good ideas here. *(Adds to his to-do list a note to create a running journal.)*"

Jack tears up his pages and notices that he feels lighter and clearer-headed. He feels more ready to start his day thinking things through and adding several to his to-do lists. He then neatens up his room before going to take a shower.

Example B

The following is an example of a Free-Form Writing process by a 58-year-old woman named Kristi, who completes this exercise every day before beginning her work as an artist:

"I feel so privileged to have time to sit and do this process for myself, and also to do the work I love everyday. Talking to Lulu the other day reminded me of how many people don't really connect with their work, and they just go through each day doing task after task they don't care about. Well, I remember what that's like, from that job I had at the mall so many years ago. Sure, it was fun and I worked with some really great people who are still friends, but it was really about the relationships and more than about the work itself. I guess if you have great people to work with, maybe the work wouldn't have to matter so much. As long as you enjoy it or it has meaning somehow. Well, what else? It's not often that my mind is empty and I have nothing to say. Haha! What do I need to do first today? Oh, I need to figure out just the right paint color for those golden hues from the sunset shining on the boat's sails. I really want the sails to look like they're glowing from within. As if the boat has a life force all its own, replying to the light emanating from the sun before it sinks below the horizon. The painting is about endings, but it's also about a journey—a journey that continues on through many endings and many new beginnings. I guess that's really a kind of renewal, when we experience an ending (even if it's sad) and then once it's over, it can't go on and something new has to start. Maybe not something to replace it exactly, but just something—instead of nothing. You really can't have "nothing" in your life or in your mind. You're always on a journey of some kind, even if it's a journey where you don't feel like you're getting anywhere. You're still moving forward in some way. Time is progressing. The clock is ticking. Your mind is not exactly the same as it was a second ago, a minute ago, or a day ago. We're changing all the time, even if it's just to note the second hand on the clock moving, or the shadows getting shorter or longer as the sun traverses the sky. Nothing ever stands still, really. It's like they say about a river—it's never the same river twice. It may look the same, but none of the water is the same water. All the water you saw there yesterday is gone, and today's is completely different water. Who knows where it came from, where each molecule has been in the course of its existence. Maybe on some distant mountain peak or in some far away ocean, or maybe just cycling between ground and sky as it falls as rain and then evaporates. There really is a lot going on, if we think about it. There's a lot of possibility. Almost infinite possibility. So many different ways to think about things and see things. Like that woman I ran into at the grocery store the other day. Her eyes caught my attention, and I felt like I knew her. A strange feeling, when I knew I'd never met her before. But there she was, and she felt like an old friend as soon as I set eyes on her. How weird is that?! What are the possibilities there? Could I have already known her somehow, from some other world or life? Or did something in her just resonate with me? Whatever it was, there was no mistaking that feeling of familiarity. Almost like I was "supposed" to know her or something. Well, anyway, it does me no good to ask why. Better to just enjoy these lovely experiences and people as they show up in my life. There is so much beauty around me, in my experiences, if I just stop and look. Just open my eyes and see with unclouded vision. I need to remember to look up from my phone or grocery list or whatever I'm focusing on and just *see* more often. See with my eyes, but also see with my intuition, my inner wisdom, my artist's eye, and my other "superpowers." It's kind of like Superman's X-ray vision—if I pay attention and look with different "eyes," I can see a

Chapter 3-22: Free-Form Writing

lot that I would miss otherwise. I can see people, who they are, and what they're about—their essences. Scenes and environments I might otherwise ignore or take for granted. Kindness, gratitude, caring, and even anger and frustration in those around me. Sometimes I get so involved in my own mind and thoughts that I forget to just look and really *see*. I'm going to set an intention to be aware of the wonders and possibilities around me in everyday life. I want to see that stranger's smile, to take in the sun dancing in the leaves of the trees, to notice the mysterious way that bumblebees stay aloft, and all the wonderful things I might otherwise miss. *(She adds to her to-do list a note about creating a new intention.)*"

Kristi feels complete, and since there isn't any more to write she shreds the free-form writing pages and carries them out to the recycling bin. On the way she notices that the grass seems even greener than yesterday, and she soaks in the warmth of the sun-warmed patio on her bare feet, while admiring a butterfly floating by on its way to a nearby flower.

Chapter 3-23
Writing a Shred Letter

This technique involves writing a letter to someone to express what's present in your consciousness—anger, blame, an apology, acknowledgment, thanks, gratitude, or anything else—and then shredding the letter instead of sending it.

When you write a shred letter, you write everything you have to say and then destroy the letter as a symbolic way of sending it—thus providing closure. You can say anything you want in this letter, because the only person who will ever see it is you. You can write a shred letter to absolutely anyone, real or imaginary. Examples include:

- Someone living or someone who has died.
- A real person you know or someone you don't know, such as a public figure.
- A historical figure, such as Leonardo da Vinci or Socrates.
- An imaginary person, such as a comic book hero or a stereotype.
- A group, institution, company, political party, cause, or social movement.
- Society, the world, or the entire universe.
- Yourself or an aspect of yourself, such as your inner child or higher wisdom.
- A character or symbol from a dream.
- A spiritual figure, according to your beliefs.

Benefits

The process of writing this letter is actually *for you.* It provides the aspects of you that need to be heard a chance to express themselves, which can sometimes be enough to resolve any underlying issues. The expression and release that happens during this process can enable deep healing of your relationship with yourself as well as your relationships with others. This is your chance to speak the unspoken, express your feelings, unburden yourself of secrets, tell your story, express gratitude, forgive, reach closure, or whatever comes forward within you. As you write, you may feel great burdens lifted as they clear from your consciousness. "Sending" the letter by shredding it provides a safe way to release the matters you've written about—and as you do, you may feel a greater peace and sense of well-being. You may also be surprised at the further shifts you notice within yourself and answers that come forward over the coming days.

The Process

The process for Writing a Shred Letter involves the following steps:

1. Sit down with pen and plenty of paper. Use paper you don't need to keep, because you're going to shred it when you're done.
2. Write the name of the person (or group or thing) to whom you have something to say.
3. Write what you want to express. Keep writing until you feel you've said everything you have to say and you feel complete, and then sign your name at the bottom.
4. Immediately destroy the letter by shredding or tearing it up as a symbolic way of sending it. This indicates to your subconscious mind that everything you've expressed has been "sent." Don't send the letter, reread it, or keep it.

Examples

Here are some examples of Writing a Shred Letter:

Example A

A young man named Evan just got home from shopping. He's feeling really frustrated with another driver who darted into a parking space that he had been waiting on for several minutes. He decides to vent his frustration in a shred letter:

"To the person who took my parking space:
"I don't think you know how I feel about what you did today in the parking lot. I had been waiting patiently for several minutes for someone to come out of the store, get in their car, and leave so I could park. You seemed to be in a big hurry, but I was too. What exactly was it that made you think your needs were more important than mine? You must have had something pretty important to get done or you wouldn't have acted so

rudely. Well, I'm not going to let your behavior ruin my day, so I'm just going to let it go. I hope you got the things done that you needed to, and I hope you calmed down so you wouldn't put anyone else through the experience I had. Sooner or later you'll probably realize that the kind of thing you did doesn't help anyone in the long run, including yourself. I hereby let go of this incident and its negative effects on me.

"*(Signed)* Evan"

Feeling relieved, Evan then shreds the letter, takes the pieces outside, and throws them in a garbage can.

Example B

A woman named Kate is recalling fond memories of her grandfather, who died several years ago. She misses talking with him and decides to write to him in a shred letter:

"Dear Grandpa Joe,

"I was just remembering all the fun we had spending time out on the lake near your farm. I didn't realize then how fortunate I was to have you as a grandfather and to get to spend time with you, just the two of us. Back then, I thought that we were just chatting aimlessly, but I actually learned some of the most important things in life from you during those talks. You were such a wise man. I still miss you so much, but most of all I feel so honored to have known you and to have had you in my life. I love you so much.

"With love and gratitude,

"*(Signed)* Kate"

She then shreds the letter as a symbolic way of sending it.

Chapter 3-24
Mental Clean-Sweep

If you're feeling overwhelmed, unclear, or having trouble focusing on what to do in your life, this Mental Clean-Sweep can help. It involves reviewing all the items on your mental to-do list, clearing out and streamlining them in a way that's more manageable and that better fits your current priorities.

Benefits

Clearing out your mental to-do list frees up mental energy. Every item on your mental to-do list continually uses a small amount of mental energy to maintain it on the list. Your subconscious mind is continuously thinking, "Oh, yeah, I still have to do that." Then when you complete the item, that bit of energy gets freed up, which you may experience as a relief or a surge of energy. This exercise can help you reclaim a lot of that mental energy by reassessing each item on your list and clearing out what's no longer needed. Similar to a reorganized closet, your mind will also become a more pleasant and functional place.

Tidying up your mental to-do list can also reduce overwhelm and sharpen your focus. An unwieldy mental to-do list can lead to a mental state that actually interferes with your ability to handle things. For example, feeling you have too much to do can lead to overwhelm that bogs down your process. This stressful state can paralyze your thinking, or it can lead to mental thrashing as you try to figure out what to do first. However, when you've cleared out unnecessary items (by delegating, deferring them to a "someday maybe" list, etc.), you'll have fewer items, a more purpose-focused list, and greater clarity about what to focus on next.

The Process

To complete a Mental Clean-Sweep, follow these steps:

1. Do a "mind dump": On paper or on your electronic device, create a list of everything you've been holding in your mind. This includes your entire mental to-do list (including any written to-do lists), all of your dreams of things you might do, become, experience, or acquire (from childhood to the present), things you have ever thought you would do someday (like travel to a certain country, learn to dance, etc.). To get more ideas, walk around your house and look in closets. Then review your life year by year to uncover more items. Continue until you can't think of any more items.
2. Sort all the items on your list into one of the following categories:

   To Do—Things you absolutely plan to do or will take steps toward in the next six months. (Transfer these items to a new "official" to-do list, and mark the top ten on which you plan to take action, starting this week.)

   Someday Maybe—Things you would perhaps like to do sometime in the future. (Use these to start a "Someday Maybe" list that you keep for future reference.)

   Done or Dropped—Things you consider to be complete enough to drop, that are no longer working for you in your life, that you no longer want to do, that don't feel on track anymore, that you are content to let other people do, or that you just choose to consider "resolved to my satisfaction." (Cross off or delete these from your list and consider them "done.")

3. Release your old list, thereby freeing up energy for your new one. You can do this by shredding your original list to symbolically release the things you choose not to hold in your mind any longer, and keeping only your new to-do and "Someday Maybe" lists. This step frees up all the mental energy you were using to hold your old to-do's, energy which is now available to focus in your chosen directions.

Example

A Mental Clean-Sweep list might look something like the following:

Chapter 3-24: Mental Clean-Sweep

- Do laundry
- Clean out bedroom closet
- Buy new car
- Learn Spanish
- Sort through old photos
- Plan family vacation
- Organize block party
- Go back to school to become a nurse
- Fix squeaky door
- Tell Mom I love her
- Try kayaking
- Replace water heater
- Plan Rachel's birthday party
- (etc.)

When you can't think of any more items, you transfer each item either to your new "To Do" list or to a "Someday Maybe" list, or cross it off if you decide to not do it. Your new lists might look like this:

To Do:
- Tell Mom I love her
- Do laundry
- Plan Rachel's birthday party
- Plan family vacation
- Call electrician
- Fix squeaky door
- Replace water heater
- Research nursing schools

Someday Maybe:
- Clean out bedroom closet
- Buy new car
- Learn Spanish
- Sort through old photos

Done or Dropped:
- Try kayaking (not interested anymore)
- Organize block party (resign from committee)

When every item on your original list has been transferred or crossed off, you shred the list as a symbolic way of releasing it from your consciousness.

Chapter 3-25
Sleep

If you think about it, you're going to be spending a certain amount of time sleeping, and if there are ways to get more benefit from those hours (such as to help you better handle and recover from stress), you have nothing to lose by trying those techniques.

Benefits

Sleep not only provides a respite from stress, the processes that occur during sleep can also bring rejuvenation and transformation on all levels. The processes that occur during sleep tend to bring healing on the physical level, and can also do so on the mental and emotional levels as you subconsciously revisit events of the day and release what no longer serves you.

Sleep can also be one of the best remedies for stress and the fatigue it brings. After a good night's sleep you might notice that your concerns from the night before seem to have lost some of their charge. You might also awaken with more clarity or an answer to yesterday's question or problem. We'll discuss many more benefits of sleep as we explore the techniques in the next section.

The Process

Your physical, mental, and emotional state can have a significant effect on sleep. For example, going to bed stressed can result in fewer hours of sleep, and the sleep you do get can be of lower quality. Shifting that internal environment at bedtime can significantly improve sleep and its benefits. Likewise, enhancing your external sleeping environment can also help ensure undisturbed, restful sleep. The following sections explore in greater detail how to enhance sleep quality and facilitate your nighttime process of rest and rejuvenation.

Preparing Your Physical Environment

Create a physical sleeping environment that is comfortable, including a supportive bed and pillow. Fresh air can also contribute to a more pleasant sleeping environment, and you may find that you sleep better in a cool environment with enough covers to be comfortably cozy. Some people enjoy sleeping with a fan running to keep the air moving, and the fan's noise itself can also facilitate sleep, as can a device that generates white noise or nature sounds.

Maintaining a clean bedroom and linens can help reduce respiratory irritation from dust and other particles. Avoid environmental toxins such as from new products like furniture, carpeting, paint, linens or other fabrics in the bedroom—as well as fumes from a nearby garage or busy street. Lingering fragrances from laundry detergent, fabric softeners, and personal care products can also cause problems for some people.

Do what you can to reduce potential interruptions to your sleep. Use the bathroom just before going to bed, make agreements with other household members to make sure you all get enough sleep, set a routine of taking your dog outside just before bedtime, and take proactive measures to avoid other interruptions wherever possible (make sure family members have water at their bedsides, etc.). Also take steps to reduce noise from the environment around you. If you can't avoid noises that wake you up, you can mask them using a device that makes a white noise, nature sounds, or other ambient sounds (but make sure they don't compromise your safety).

Make the room where you sleep as dark as possible. Turn off all lights and cover any windows that let light in. However, beware of room-darkening curtains or shades with a toxic chemical coating. You might also want to consider a motion-sensor nightlight that only turns on when it senses movement in the room.

Wear loose, comfortable clothing to sleep in. Choose garments that don't restrict your movements and that won't cause you to overheat. If you get cold you can add more covers, and you won't have to get up and change your clothing of you get too warm in the middle of the night.

Preparing Your Body

The physical factors within your body can also affect your mental and emotional state, thereby affecting your sleep and dreams. Therefore, you may want to make a point of eating a healthy diet and avoiding problem substances that can lead to Toxic Dreams ("Toxic Dreams," p. 154) and interfere with good quality sleep, such as toxic chemicals, sugar, caffeine, alcohol, tobacco, and other psychoactive substances. Also, avoid using computers or other electronic devices during the hour or so before bedtime to enhance your transition into sleep mode.

Elevating Your Consciousness

Elevating your inner state before you fall asleep can improve your sleep, enhance your dreams, and help you fall asleep more quickly. The following techniques can be very effective in shifting your conscious awareness upward toward soul and into a higher quality sleep experience.

Call in the Light

Calling in the light only takes a moment and has long-lasting effects ("Calling in the Light," p. 17). When you call in the light to fill, surround, and protect you for the highest good of all concerned, the light stays with you throughout the night. You receive its direct benefit as well as the peace of mind that comes with sleeping within the protection and action of the light.

Spiritual Exercises

Spiritual exercises can help you elevate above the lower levels of worries and mental chatter, clear the way for whatever healing and transformation will be available during sleep, and improve sleep quality and dream content, among many other wonderful benefits ("Chapter 3-18: Spiritual Exercises," p. 114).

Meditation

Various forms of meditation can calm you and release mental chatter, especially if you choose a type of meditation that elevates your consciousness, is soothing, and focuses on peace ("Chapter 3-21: Meditation," p. 124).

Prayer

A bedtime prayer can provide the obvious positive results of whatever you're praying for, as well as effects beyond what you're imagining or hoping for ("Chapter 4-5: Prayer," p. 169). The simple act of intentionally connecting into the Divine can bring the immediate benefits of higher consciousness and releasing of negativity and disturbances. In your prayer, you might ask that the Divine (or whatever name with which you feel comfortable) be with you throughout the night and provide perfect healing, clarity, upliftment, or whatever is for your highest good right now. Examples include:

- "I place everyone and everything into the light for the highest good of all concerned."
- "I ask tonight for the Divine to handle all that I'm concerned about, and to resolve and heal what can be resolved and healed in a way that's for the highest good of all concerned."

Gratitude

Practicing gratitude before you fall asleep can also shift your inner state upward ("Chapter 4-14: Gratitude," p. 184). You can simply list inwardly what you're grateful or thankful for, and keep going until you run out of things or you drift off to sleep.

Send the Light

At bedtime sending the light to others is another way to move into the unconditional loving of soul, and it can also bring about a deep sense of peace and calm within you ("Sending the Light," p. 19). Simply say inwardly, "Light to Mario" or "Light to all those suffering" or "Light to all beings" or wherever you want the light to go. Keep listing them until you feel complete or fall asleep.

Dealing with Emotions and Mental Chatter

If you're experiencing stress, strong emotion, or mental chatter, it's a good idea to work through it before going to sleep. If something specific is bothering you, address it before going to sleep if that's possible, or at least decide to set it aside until you wake up tomorrow. For example, you might offload all the mental to-do items from your consciousness by writing them down. If your mind is going a mile a minute, you might do some free-form writing to allow it to have its say ("Chapter 3-22: Free-Form Writing," p. 127). If you're feeling scattered you could do a centering technique ("Chapter 4-2: Centering," p. 165).

If you're feeling particularly emotionally charged (such as angry, frustrated, or afraid), look to the factors underlying that emotion. Emotion is often part of a reaction to or interpretation of an internal or external event. The emotion often rides on a mental dynamic such as a belief, judgment, imagined scenario, expectation, or decision. For example, a fear that you might become ill may be based on an imagined scenario of becoming ill and possibly an irrational belief that "I'm going to catch an illness and die from it." Anger at the world for not being a better place could be based on an inaccurate belief that "The world is a horrible place" and a judgment of the world as "bad" or "wrong."

If you need more clarity about the factors underlying the emotion, process through the emotion as described in "Chapter 3-4: Processing Emotions" (p. 58), and look for more clues in "Stress Comes from Within" (p. 15), "Chapter 3-5: Forgiveness" (p. 61), "Chapter 3-6: Reframing" (p. 65), "Chapter 3-7: Transforming Beliefs" (p. 68), and "Chapter 3-11: Revisiting Past Decisions" (p. 85).

Calming Yourself

If you've tried the previous techniques in this chapter and you're still feeling keyed up when it's time for sleep, explore following additional techniques to calm both body and mind.

- Deep breathing or focused breathing ("Chapter 4-23: Focused Breathing," p. 199).
- Visualization ("Chapter 4-15: Visualization," p. 185, and especially "Chapter 3-19: Rainbow Visualization," p. 118).
- Soothing music or sounds ("Chapter 4-30: Music," p. 210).

Setting Your Focus

Bedtime is a powerful time to plant any "seeds" within your consciousness that you'd like to take root during the night. You can do this using tools such as intentions and affirmations.

Pre-Sleep Intentions

You can create a pre-sleep intention ("Chapter 3-8: Setting Intentions," p. 71) to define a particular experience or result you'd like to create, such as:

- "I intend to lift into the awareness of soul tonight."
- "I intend to rest well and awaken into greater peace."
- "I intend to release and heal that which is available to be released and healed within me for the highest good."
- "I intend to be open to any beneficial insights that come forward during the night."

Pre-Sleep Affirmations

Just before you fall asleep is a great time to repeat your affirmation ("Chapter 3-20: Affirmations," p. 120) if you've been working with one, or you can create a new one. Examples include:

- "I am centering in soul and I'm open to any healing that's available."
- "I am accepting what is and I place all in the light for the highest good."
- "I am centering in peace, living fully each day, and resting well each night."
- "I am replenishing each night and nurturing myself each day."

If Sleep Is Interrupted

If you wake up and can't fall back to sleep, consider what might be keeping you awake. For example, if your mind is racing or you're feeling strong emotion, you might try the bedtime techniques in "Dealing with Emotions and Mental Chatter" (p. 141). If you woke up from a nightmare, you may need to diffuse its negative effects (see "Chapter 3-27: Dealing with

Nightmares," p. 153). There could also be a physical or biological factor at play, such as something you ate or drank too close to bedtime, in which case you can try the techniques in "Elevating Your Consciousness" (p. 140) and "Calming Yourself" (p. 142) while you're giving yourself time to feel better physically. If your mind feels wide awake, you might engage your mind (such as by reading, journaling, or listening to a podcast—but stay away from devices with lighted displays, which can keep you from getting sleepy) until you start to feel sleepy again. However, if you simply don't feel sleepy, you might try the Rainbow Visualization (see "Chapter 3-19: Rainbow Visualization," p. 118).

When Waking Up

When you wake up and before opening your eyes, review any dreams from beginning to end and decide whether to interpret them ("Chapter 3-26: Dream Interpretation," p. 144). If you had a nightmare, take steps to recover from it and clear any residual negativity ("Chapter 3-27: Dealing with Nightmares," p. 153).

Before getting out of bed is a great time to create your focus for the coming day. For example, you might repeat an affirmation ("Chapter 3-20: Affirmations," p. 120) or set an intention for the day ("Chapter 3-8: Setting Intentions," p. 71).

Now is also the perfect opportunity to positively affect the quality and experience of the day by elevating your consciousness and centering in soul. Even just five minutes of spiritual exercises ("Chapter 3-18: Spiritual Exercises," p. 114) and a quick centering process ("Chapter 4-2: Centering," p. 165) can improve your whole day.

Chapter 3-26
Dream Interpretation

Dreams can be sources of powerful, life-transforming information if you pay attention to their meanings. They provide glimpses of yourself and your life that you might not otherwise see: your deepest desires, untapped potential, self-defeating patterns, and opportunities for greater happiness. Locked within your dreams are empowering insights, waiting to be discovered like your own personal buried treasure.

Because dream meanings are individual to each person, you must look within yourself to find true dream meaning. Although you may look to external sources for ideas about possible meanings, ultimately you must look inward and rely on your own intuition to confirm dream meaning.

(This chapter provides an overview of dream interpretation. You can find more in-depth information in my other books, *The Curious Dreamer's Practical Guide to Dream Interpretation* (more on p. 219) and *The Curious Dreamer's Dream Dictionary* (more on p. 220).

The Goal of Dream Interpretation
The practical goal of dream interpretation, as I see it, is to find the value in each dream so you can then apply it to improve yourself and your life. A dream's value may be profound and life changing, or as simple as the realization that eating sweets too close to bedtime can trigger nightmares. Whatever the content of a dream, you can learn from it.

Intuition: Your Dream Translator
Your intuition is your own personal translator of the language of dream symbolism. Intuition is key in understanding dream meaning because it's the part of you that recognizes truth.

Each dream could potentially have many different possible meanings. The logical mind can analyze a dream and suggest a variety of potential meanings, but the challenge is recognizing the true meaning when you see it. Perhaps you'll come across the true meaning while you're reviewing your dream, when you're trying different analysis techniques, while you're discussing the dream with a friend, or at some other point. You could use every approach there is and still not know which meaning is correct, until you recognize it intuitively.

Only *you* can definitively recognize the true meaning of your dream. I use the word "recognize" because identifying dream meaning doesn't involve rational knowing. Dream interpretation simply involves using the conscious mind to explore different possible meanings until one resonates with what you already know—when your intuition tells you, "Yes! That's what the dream means." This recognition of dream meaning is what I call *dream intuition.* In practice, dream intuition is the use of intuition in the dream interpretation process.

Although intuition tends to be continuously active, it may not always be clear and obvious to you. The greatest challenge with intuition is that it can easily be confused with or drowned out by other factors within your consciousness—thoughts, fears, stresses, hopes, judgments, memories, imaginings, daydreams, and so on. With all that other activity in your mind, you may not be able to discern intuition—which tends to show up as quiet and neutral, rather than demanding your attention.

Intuition can be obscured when you mistake one of those other mental or emotional factors as being your intuition and focus on it instead. When a particular idea enters your consciousness, you may not be able to tell whether it's an intuitive insight or another factor you're mistaking for intuitive truth. This isn't to say that those other factors don't have value, because they can have. However, they are not intuition and they should not be taken as such. Discerning intuition from other factors is a skill that can be developed through practice, as discussed in "Follow Your Intuition (Sometimes)" (p. 30).

Dreams Are About You

Because dreams occur within a deep part of yourself, it's not surprising that most of what they convey pertains to yourself and your life.

Dreams Tell About You and Your Life

Dreams very often portray a snapshot of some part of your daily life or something on your mind, presented from the perspective of (and in the language of) your subconscious mind. As you examine each dream, you can often find a parallel between each element in the dream and a certain element of your waking life or mind.

Dreams Show Your Perspective
In most dreams, everything in the dream (all the elements, people, settings, etc.) pertains to you personally. More specifically, most dreams portray your thoughts and feelings about things, rather than portraying the things themselves. Each dream symbol tends to represent your perspective of something from real life, rather than the actual thing. For example, your sister in a dream likely portrays your experience of her (rather than her, herself), your perception of something she said (rather than what she actually said or meant), or your assumption about what she was thinking (rather than her actual thoughts).

Dreams Convey a Distorted Reality
Because dreams portray people and things the way you view or interpret them, you can't rely on a dream for an accurate representation of reality. Every dream has been filtered through the distorting lens of your subconscious mind and often infused with subconscious fears, desires, and imaginings. Therefore, it's unwise to base a decision solely on a dream, which would mean blindly following the whims of your subconscious mind.

Consider Common Dream Symbolism First
If there's any such thing as a shortcut to finding dream meaning, this is it. The majority of dreams convey meaning using one of just a few forms of symbolism. So, chances are that your dream symbol represents something in your life or mind in one of the following ways, which you'll begin to recognize as you interpret more dreams. When searching for a symbol's meaning, always consider these most common forms of symbolism first.

Literal Translation
If the dream symbol (person, event, object, action, setting, etc.) exists in your real life, it might represent that actual element of your life. For example, your mother hugging you might represent a certain time she hugged you, or her affection for you in general. When a symbol represents the same thing in your current life, past, or imagined future, here's a clue: your dream feelings will likely feel similar to your real-life feelings.

Emotions
The emotions you feel regarding the dream symbol are probably the same as the emotions you feel about whatever the symbol represents in your real life. For example, if you feel overwhelmed by a swarm of insects in a dream, the swarm might represent your to-do list that feels overwhelming in real life.

Chapter 3-26: Dream Interpretation

Abundance or Lack

A dream symbol can represent something that you feel you have too much of, do too much of, or want less of in your real life. Alternatively, your dream symbol could represent something that you feel you lack, do too little of, or want more of. If your dream contained a pleasant experience (such as relaxing on a beach), your subconscious mind could be pointing to your desire for more pleasantness in your life. If your dream was unpleasant (such as someone judging you), your subconscious mind may have been focused on trying to avoid that kind of experience in real life.

Personal Symbolism

A dream symbol may convey meaning that you personally associate with it based on your experiences, feelings, and other influences. For example, one person might associate a baby with vulnerability and someone else might associate it with growth.

A particular dream symbol may bring more than one meaning to mind for you. For example, money might bring to mind how fun money is to spend, but you might also think of money as power or as a solution to financial problems. If the first meaning that comes to mind doesn't seem to relate to anything in your real life and doesn't resonate intuitively, explore additional meanings.

Importance

The symbols you tend to notice in a dream are often the most important ones. So a good place to start when exploring your dream is with the symbols that stood out. Symbols may stand out because they're so huge you can't miss them (like a boulder falling on your house) or they could be small details that happen to stand out in your mind (like the chipped rim of a teacup). Sometimes an important symbol is highlighted in the dream with a bright color, illuminated with light, pointed to with an arrow, or emphasized in some other way.

Urgency

If there's a sense of urgency involved in the dream, the dream might represent an urgent matter that you feel needs attention in your real life (or one that you fear or imagine needs attention). For example, a dream about trying to put out a fire at work could point to a real-life problem that arose suddenly at work that you feel requires quick action to avoid catastrophe.

Subject Context

A dream might be about you or it could represent your perception of a friend or a recent situation—even in the media, on TV, or in a movie. For example, in a dream about a girl wearing a cheerful flowered dress, the girl could represent a happier version of yourself or your desire to feel more cheerful. Alternatively, she might represent a friend who was in a happy mood when you saw her yesterday, an upbeat song you just heard, or an optimistic character you saw in a TV show last night.

Time Context
A dream symbol could represent something in your past, present, or imagined future. Look for elements that bring to mind a particular time frame, either in the characteristics of the symbol itself or in the other things associated with it in the dream (people, activities, clothes, places, music, books, etc.). Time-related cues could include things like hair or clothing styles, a person appearing younger or older than their current age in real life, technologies of a different era, or personal cues such as the cowboy boots you wore at age seven.

Emotional Exaggeration
When a dream portrays a real-life situation that's particularly emotional for the dreamer, sometimes the situation shows up as exaggerated in the dream. In other words, the subconscious mind may amplify the real-life situation, "making a mountain out of a molehill," expressing how strongly the dreamer feels about the dream's subject matter. For example, if in real life you saw a baby snake in your yard, and you're very afraid of snakes, the snake might show up in a dream as a huge serpent attacking you. So, consider whether a particular dream symbol could represent a similar but less extreme situation in your waking life, about which you feel strong emotion.

Benefits

One dream can change your life if you understand its meaning. When you focus on finding the value in your dreams, virtually every dream provides something meaningful that can help you improve your life or your state of being. For example, dreams can point the way out of old patterns and into new opportunity. They can reveal solutions to problems in your personal relationships. Dreams can also suggest changes in your way of thinking to create a less stressful environment within yourself. When you translate dream meaning, it can help you:

- Better understand yourself and your needs.
- Get answers to important questions.
- Clarify life purpose and direction.
- Discover creative ideas and visions.
- Help resolve issues from the past.
- Uncover self-limiting dynamics within.

- Resolve fears and move ahead.
- Reduce stress in your day-to-day life.
- Identify important health conditions.
- Detect and resolve blocks to inner peace.
- Remove obstacles to experiencing soul.

The Process

To interpret a dream and apply what you learn from it to improve your life, these four steps can yield surprisingly powerful results:

1. **Review Your Dream**—Upon awakening from your dream, before opening your eyes, replay your dream in your mind from beginning to end as if you are mentally replaying a movie you've just seen. This process helps to pull the whole thread of your dream out of your subconscious mind and into your conscious memory so you can remember its details later. (If you skip this step, the dream may stay trapped in your subconscious mind once you're fully awake, and you may not remember much.)

2. **Record Your Dream**—Write a description of your dream, preferably right after you open your eyes while the details are still fresh. Once your dream is written down, you have the option to come back to it later. A written description gives you something to refer to later and add notes to as you interpret the dream. Also, the writing process itself may trigger your memory of more dream details. I strongly recommend writing your dream description on paper, where you can draw pictures and write notes, rather than on a computer or other device.

3. **Analyze Your Dream**—Once you've written your dream description, you're ready to begin interpreting it. I think of **dream interpretation** as assigning meaning to a dream or its parts. Dream interpretation can include dream analysis (the systematic examination of a dream, such as a logical assessment of its symbolism and structure) as well as subjective assessment and non-mental dynamics such as intuition and emotions. I think of **dream analysis** as a structured process that provides various ways to look at the dream through your mind's eye, until your intuition says "Yes! That's the meaning of this dream." The dream analysis process involves both your rational mind and your intuition simultaneously. Sometimes your intuition will confirm the dream's true meaning right away. Other times, you may need to help the intuitive process along by spending more time with the dream, looking at it from various

angles using different analysis techniques, and finding ways to quiet your mind so you can hear your intuition.
4. **Act on Your Dream**—Once you understand your dream's meaning, consider what (if any) action to take based on the content of the dream. You now have an opportunity to act on what you learned, to apply the information from your dream in a positive way. Consider what your dream conveyed about what's working and what's not in your life, and any other opportunities to improve yourself and your life. This could mean taking action within your own consciousness, such as releasing judgments, replacing self-defeating beliefs, renegotiating outdated agreements with yourself, finding closure on situations from the past, or clarifying life direction. You might also see opportunities for external follow-up actions, such as solving a problem, trying something new, identifying and acting on your strengths, or completing an unfinished project.

Here are some examples of the many follow-up actions you might take to improve yourself and your life based on information from your dreams:

- Accept yourself, someone else, or a situation in your life.
- Forgive a past action.
- Release limiting beliefs.
- Address or heal emotional wounds.
- Find closure and peace by working through your feelings about the past.
- Release life situations that are no longer working for you.
- Create more of what you want, and less of what you don't want.
- Solve a problem or work through a challenge.
- Catalyze a creative process.
- Clarify your life direction.
- Identify your strengths and gifts.
- Deepen your spirituality.

Examples

The following examples illustrate how a person might interpret and apply a particular dream:

Example A

Imagine you dreamed that you were driving at night in an old car, when suddenly the steering failed, causing you to drive off the road. In Step 1 you determine that the car was the main symbol in this dream, and in Step 2 you summarize what stood out about the car as "An old car I was driving that went out of control." In Step 3 you look for parallels between aspects of the dream and aspects of your waking life. First, you describe your feelings during the dream as "I felt panic when I couldn't control the car and I was afraid of crashing." You realize that you recognize this feeling from your waking life—similar to the panic and out-of-control feeling regarding your finances lately, your fear of financial disaster. You describe the physical car symbol as "The car was old, rusty and in need of maintenance"—which you suspect may refer to your spending patterns that could use an overhaul. You describe the car's setting as "The car was traveling on a winding road"—which could represent an unpredictable process or journey somewhere in your life. You characterize the car's environment as "The car was driving at night"—which you suspect could imply something happening without your awareness—something about which you're "in the dark." You summarize the actions involving the car as "The car's steering stopped working and the car veered off the road and crashed"—which you think represents the time in real life when you stopped making wise decisions about spending, after which you experienced financial crisis. You don't see any obvious wordplay, so you move on to Step 4, in which you review your observations and explore the patterns that show parallels between your dream and your real life. When you review each dream element, your intuition jumps to the aspect of your waking life to which it refers. You recognize the out-of-control feeling in the car as similar to your out-of-control feelings about your finances. Veering off the winding road in the dark when the steering stopped working seems to represent your real life situation of poor decision making in the face of unpredictable financial demands, represented by the winding road. This is a pattern of which you've been unaware ("in the dark" about) until now, represented in the dream by the dark setting. The car needing maintenance seems to represent your financial patterns and decision making which need some attention and updating. You conclude that this dream portrays what you've been experiencing in the financial area of your life and the financial trouble that may occur if you don't take corrective action in that area.

Example B

Imagine you dreamed that a bee was pestering you. In Step 1, you identify the key symbol as the bee, and in Step 2 you summarize what immediately stood out about it as "The bee kept buzzing around my face." Looking for parallels with your real life in Step 3, you note that during the dream you experienced feelings of fear that the bee would sting you and frustration because it wouldn't leave you alone. You recognize these feelings as similar to a real life situation in which you're afraid of someone who has been pestering you at school. You note the bee's physical characteristic of being bigger than usual, which could imply a pest that "looms large" in your life or has a big effect on you. You note the bee's setting as the inside of your house—which could mean that whatever the bee represents has intruded into your personal space. You note the environment in which the bee appeared was during the daytime while you were trying to get things done—which could represent the idea of something that interferes with your day-to-day activities. You note the actions of the bee, which seemed to be taunting you, repeatedly flying near your face—which could represent someone repeatedly taunting or pestering you at school. You note the possible wordplay—a bee is a type of "bug"—so perhaps it represents something that is "bugging" you. In Step 4 you review your observations and conclude that the bee in the dream represents a girl at school who has been pestering you, intruding into your space when you are trying to focus on your schoolwork. She is relentless, and you are afraid that taking any action against her will result in you getting in trouble—getting "stung." You realize that this dream illustrates the situation from your waking life, but it does not provide any answer about what to do about it. So, you decide to talk it over with someone you trust to give you good advice, and then make a decision about what action to take.

Chapter 3-27
Dealing with Nightmares

Most people have nightmares or other upsetting dreams at least occasionally. A variety of physical, mental, and emotional factors may play a role in precipitating these kinds of dreams. When you experience a nightmare, you might want to consider possible underlying factors such as the following:

- Some nightmares are Toxic Dreams, which are typically very realistic and upsetting dreams that occur in response to certain kinds of foods, drugs, or toxins, or in times of physical, mental, or emotional stress (read more about this dream type in "Toxic Dreams," p. 154).
- Nightmares may occur when the subconscious mind plays out subconscious fears or rehearses worst-case scenarios during the dream state. It's possible in these cases that the subconscious mind is trying to prepare in order to avoid or to better handle a scary situation in real life.
- Experiencing an unpleasant event in real life—or in a TV show, movie, book, video game, or other alternate reality—can also trigger a nightmare.
- Nightmares can be triggered by the lingering effects of past trauma in real life. If this is the case, the nightmare may be pointing to an opportunity for deeper healing, a process for which you might consider seeking the guidance of a trusted mental health professional.
- A nightmare can also occur when a person has abandoned responsibility for himself or his own well-being. For example, engaging in activities such as overeating sweets or consuming a large amount of alcohol can be ways of abandoning responsibility for yourself that open the door for nightmares to occur (read more in "Toxic Dreams," p. 154).

- Allowing a "negative cloud" to perpetuate within your consciousness can also lead to nightmares. Dark emotions and negative inner influences often indicate a matter within yourself that needs your attention, which you can address using techniques such as the ones in "Part III: Haven-Building Toolkit" (p. 35).

Toxic Dreams

A Toxic Dream is triggered by a toxic state, in which you are physically, mentally, or emotionally overloaded during sleep. Toxic Dreams are usually very realistic and upsetting dreams. They can be terrible nightmares. Often, having a Toxic Dream simply indicates that you were in a toxic state at the time of the dream, more than providing any useful meaning to interpret. These dreams can result from a number of factors occurring the day or evening before, including:

- Eating refined carbohydrates (such as sweets or white flour), processed or junk food, additives, or preservatives.
- Eating too much, especially close to bedtime.
- Ingesting drugs, alcohol, caffeine, tobacco, or other substances that are psychoactive or that stress or overload the body.
- Taking certain prescription medications, or changing your dose (consult your doctor if you suspect this is an issue).
- Eating foods to which you have a sensitivity or allergy (common culprits are wheat, gluten, dairy, soy, nuts, eggs, and corn).
- Encountering environmental toxins (such as from mold, new carpet, cleaning chemicals, or exhaust fumes).
- Being stressed (the biochemical results of stress can overload the body, as external toxins can).
- Being emotionally toxic, such as going to bed angry or hateful.
- Not getting enough rest (sleep deprivation can deny the body its critical nighttime detoxing, leaving more toxins in the body).
- Being ill or otherwise not feeling well.

Often Toxic Dreams are nightmares that play upon your subconscious fears. Here are some examples:

You have been very stressed the last three days and haven't slept well for the last week. You dreamed that you seriously injured yourself in a household accident, but that when you picked up the phone and dialed 911 you kept getting the wrong number and couldn't get through. This dream may indicate a feeling of helplessness, possibly due to an underlying feeling that your life is out of control due to your recent stressful situation. On a physical level, your body may have been overwhelmed by stress-related biochemicals and an overstimulated condition, creating an extra challenge during the sleep cycle. To avoid this situation, you might apply some stress management techniques such as delegating or reorganizing your tasks to reduce your stress load, free-form writing to get out your frustrations, or meditation and visualization.

You ate a large piece of pie just before going to bed, and you dreamed that a monster was coming after you and inflicted serious physical harm on you. This dream may point to a subconscious fear of being victimized, but the main significance is the physical state of overload while the body was going through its sleep cycle. To avoid this situation, you might avoid carbohydrate-intense foods and avoid eating so close to bedtime.

Recovering from a Nightmare

When dealing with "problem dreams" such as nightmares and Toxic Dreams, the idea is to glean any value from these dreams that you can, and then release them so that they no longer affect your subconscious or waking consciousness. Recovery from such a dream involves redirecting your consciousness away from the dream setting, recovering emotionally, and removing mental and emotional residues left behind by the dream. The best time to begin your recovery is immediately after waking up from the dream. Helpful techniques include:

- Visualization or meditation to lift yourself out of the negative state ("Chapter 3-19: Rainbow Visualization," p. 118, is particularly helpful).
- Banish the negative dream elements from your internal environment (you are the master of your domain).
- Detach from the dream (see "Detach from the Dream," p. 156).
- Recreate the ending of the dream to make the outcome more positive (see "Rewrite the Dream in Your Mind," p. 157).
- Do a reality check by acknowledging the physical reality around you (see "Do a Reality Check," p. 160).

Nightmares can be interpreted using the same techniques as other dreams—looking for parallels with situations in the dreamer's real life, but paying special attention to possible links to subconscious fears and recent traumatic experiences (either real or virtual, such as watching a movie). However, if a nightmare was a Toxic Dream, it may simply have been triggered by your toxic state at the time of the dream, and therefore it may offer no useful meaning to interpret.

Benefits

By dealing with the effects of a nightmare as soon as you wake up, you can minimize its unpleasant effects while gaining whatever value you can from its content. More specifically, following up after a nightmare can help you:

- Recover from the disturbances experienced during the nightmare.
- Remove lingering emotional residues.
- Release the influences of the dream that no longer serve you.
- Elevate your consciousness out of the "scary level."
- Resolve any unresolved issues your dream brought up.
- Bring to light any subconscious fears so they can be addressed.
- Take control of the dream narrative by retelling the story in an uplifting way.

The Process

The following sections present three techniques for recovering from a nightmare: "Detach from the Dream," "Rewrite the Dream in Your Mind," and "Do a Reality Check."

Detach from the Dream

This technique is intended to help get a nightmare out of your system—to remove its effects from your consciousness, to empty them out of your mind, emotions, subconscious mind, and all other aspects of you. You can complete this technique with eyes open or closed, but some people find the visualization easier with eyes closed.

1. Call in the light (see "Calling in the Light," p. 17).
2. Send love to and release all judgments against all who were involved in the dream. This step is just as much for your sake as for theirs, so that your judgments or grudges do not lock the negativity of the dream into your consciousness. If you can't bring yourself to send love and forgiveness, then send thoughts that you hope all involved will be healed, filled with love, and become kinder.
3. Release the dream, the dream location and characters, and all negativity associated with it. One way to do this is to say inwardly, "I release this dream, its location and characters, and any negative residues from it."

4. Visualize the whole dream leaving you and floating into the light. Alternatively, visualize the dream leaving your body and floating into a Divine white flame, where it disperses on contact.

Examples

Here are some examples of using this process to Detach from a Dream:

Example A

After waking from a nightmare about a very tall woman trying to harm you, you begin by calling in the light. You then send love to and release judgments of all involved in the dream, including to the woman and to the "you" who was in the dream. You immediately feel the negativity within you begin to dissipate. Next, you release the entire dream by saying, "I release this dream and any negative residues from it into the light," and you observe as the dream disappears completely and its effects flow out of your consciousness into the light.

Example B

Consider a nightmare in which your house was on fire and you were trying to phone for help, but you couldn't press the right buttons on the phone. After you awaken you call in the light, and then you send love to all involved in the dream, including yourself. You release the dream by saying, "I release this entire dream and any negative residues from it," and you visualize the entire dream leaving your body and dissolving in a Divine white flame.

Rewrite the Dream in Your Mind

A dream can leave you feeling a certain way when it's over, just as movie leaves you in a particular mental or emotional state at the end. Using the following technique, you can change your inner state by "rewriting" the ending of your dream in a more positive way, to resolve any outstanding issues and tie up any loose ends. In other words, you can give your dream a happy ending. For example, in a dream that ended with you falling off a bridge into a river, you could visualize the story continuing with a large air cushion deploying below you, on which you land safely. Re-envisioning the outcome this way can help release any emotional distress you are still feeling and shift into a more positive state.

1. Close your eyes and visualize the last thing that happened in your dream.

2. Create the rest of the story, giving it any ending you choose. Imagine that you're watching the rest of the movie, and give it a positive ending with a satisfying resolution. I suggest using positive, win-win strategies rather than lowering yourself into negativity and creating more negativity within your consciousness. Examples of positive strategies include:

Send Love—Shoot love or peace toward your attacker until his negativity is dissolved. For example, imagine using a Ghostbusters-type gun that drenches the attacker with pure love—or a peace-breathing dragon who breathes out peace instead of fire—which not only stops the attacker in his tracks, but also fills him with love or peace.

Disarm With Humor—Imagine that a purple polka-dot cow flies in and eats your attacker's weapon or chases him away, or imagine your attacker wearing huge clown shoes and a big red nose and doing a silly dance off into the sunset.

Bring in a Helper—Imagine a source of help neutralizing the negative element in the dream. You can imagine any figure—past, present, or created in your mind—stepping in and neutralizing the negativity in the dream through positive action. For example, you might imagine a superhero surrounding your attacker in a cloud of pure love—or a fairy godmother waving her magic wand—and the negativity then drains from him.

Eject the Negative—Tell the attacker that it must leave. Say something like "You are not allowed here. This was my dream, this is my consciousness, and I am in charge. You must leave now." Then envision white light filling your consciousness and pushing him out of it.

Lift Above—Imagine yourself climbing into a beautiful hot air balloon and being lifted up out of the scene and into a bright, white, light cloud of love and peace, or imagine that by generating love within yourself you can levitate upward and float away to a peaceful place.

Rewind and Redirect—Rewind the dream story by envisioning everything happening quickly in reverse until you get to a point before a problem developed. Then play the story forward, but this time redirect the story your way—in a positive way. For example, you might rewind a dream in which someone steals your wallet, and redirect it to tell a story in which you deploy a protective rubber bubble around yourself, which the would-be thief just bounces off of when he tries to approach you.

Examples

The following examples show how you might Rewrite the Dream in Your Mind to help disperse the effects of a nightmare:

Example A

Imagine a dream in which a mean man was chasing you and was just about to catch you, and then you woke up. Upon awakening, you close your eyes and visualize the last moment of the dream, when he was close enough to touch you. You then visualize another ending to the dream—one in which you dissolve his negativity with love. You visualize yourself pivoting around and "shooting love" at him through your eyes—bright white love, inundating him with caring and goodwill. You feel yourself actually wanting him to become kind, to be healed of whatever emotional wound has brought out the meanness in him. As the love engulfs him, you visualize it replacing the meanness within him, and the angry expression on his face is replaced with one of kindness and relief. Now he is a grateful, happy guy. You visualize him thanking you for helping him and then going on his way until he fades from view.

Example B

Consider a nightmare in which you're adrift in a small inflatable boat in the middle of the ocean, when a storm begins tossing you on huge waves. The boat then loses air and begins taking on water. A huge wave is towering over you, ready to crash, when you wake up. You close your eyes and visualize yourself in the sinking boat. Then you visualize an ending to the dream in which the sky suddenly clears, the storm clouds are replaced with happy, fluffy clouds, and the waters become calm. Then a hot air balloon floats down from above. You climb into its basket, and you feel an overwhelming sense of love and well-being. The balloon begins lifting—and the higher it goes, the greater your sense of love and well-being. You close your eyes, feel the warm sun on your face, and enjoy the experience.

Do a Reality Check

One of the reasons that nightmares are so disturbing is that they tend to feel so real. Otherwise, we wouldn't respond to them in such an extreme emotional way. If the subconscious mind experiences the events in a nightmare as a reality, you may be able to erase the nightmare's effects by doing a reality check—by proving to your subconscious mind that the nightmare is not your current reality. You can do this by replacing the dream reality with your current waking reality. You might find that the most effective way to do this is visually and through your other senses, by "showing your subconscious mind" a physical reality that is different from the one in the nightmare.

Examples

The following examples illustrate how you might Do a Reality Check to counteract lingering impressions from a nightmare:

Example A

Perhaps you dreamed that your mother died in a car crash. You might do a reality check to erase this nightmare from your consciousness by "showing your subconscious mind" that your mother is alive and well by calling, visiting, or video-chatting with her. This waking version of reality conflicts with and replaces the nightmare version of reality.

Example B

Imagine that you woke up from a nightmare about enemy planes dropping bombs on your house during the night. You might do a reality check by "showing your subconscious mind" that:

- It is daytime (not nighttime), by noticing the daylight shining into your room.
- There are no planes flying over your house, by looking out the window at the empty sky and listening to the silence.
- Your house is intact, by walking around and viewing the intact structure.
- There are no reports of any bombings in your area, by checking the news on TV or the internet.

PART IV
QUICK-FIX TOOLKIT

About This Toolkit

Each technique in this section offers an "umbrella in the storm" for a temporary respite from stress. You can use these techniques to relieve stress in any moment until you can find an opportunity later to transform the underlying dynamics of your stress reaction so the stress trigger can no longer affect you (such as by using the first 17 techniques in "Part III: Haven-Building Toolkit," p. 35). The techniques here can also help dissipate residual effects of stress after you've transformed the underlying dynamics.

Before using these techniques, be sure you've read "Chapter 2-2: Using the Techniques in This Book" (p. 27).

Chapter 4-1
Calling in the Light (Quick Version)

Calling in the light is an all-purpose remedy in any situation, including stressful ones. This versatile tool can bring immediate peace and can actually help shift the situation that's triggering your stress. When you say, "Light for the highest good of all concerned," you surround yourself and the situation with light, and you also invoke an "insurance policy" for everything to happen in the best way for everyone involved, even taking into account all the things you have no way of knowing. (You can read much more about how and when to call in the light in "Calling in the Light," p. 17.)

Chapter 4-2
Centering

Centering is one of the quickest and most effective ways to shift out of a stressful state. The idea is to elevate your consciousness by focusing into a higher level, such as soul or the Divine. As you do that, your awareness lifts above any stress you were experiencing and into greater peace. This process can also help transform the underlying dynamics of your stressful reaction through the action of allowing the light to enter those areas of disturbance.

Centering in Soul

To center in soul, inwardly or outwardly make one of the following centering statements (or create your own):

- "I center in soul."
- "I am soul."
- "I bring my awareness into the peace of soul."
- "As a soul, I open to the profound peace and love within."
- "I bring my entire being into soul accord."

For more about soul and how to center in soul, see "Getting to Soul" (p. 7).

Centering in the Divine

To center in the Divine (or the "highest power," or other name of your choosing), inwardly or outwardly say one of the following (or something similar):

- "I center in the Divine."
- "I call myself forward to the Divine."
- "I open to the Divine and allow it to fill all aspects of me."
- "I center in the Divine and ask for Divine light to fill, surround, and protect me for the highest good of all concerned."
- "I bring forward the Divine into all that I am and all that I do."

Expanded Centering Statements

You can used longer, more details centering statements with multiple aspects to assist upward movement, combining concepts such as light, love, peace, healing, releasing, and higher wisdom. For example:

- "I consecrate and bless all that is within. I confirm love and life within all of my being. I invite Divine light to fill my being, cleanse all that no longer serves me, transform all that no longer uplifts me, and reach into all areas of darkness and allow them to fill with Divine light. I am at one with the Divine and I am at peace."
- "I shift my awareness to the beautiful soul that I am, celebrating the perfect essence of my being. I acknowledge that as a soul I am perfect and I am whole. All is well within me and I am at peace. I invite peace to permeate all aspects of my being."

Power in Repetition

The most powerful centering statement is one that resonates deeply with you and leads your consciousness into a more elevated state. Once you've chosen a statement that works well for you, you can use often so it becomes like a touchstone, becoming more effective over time as it repeatedly assists your consciousness in creating a familiar, well-worn path for upward movement.

Chapter 4-3
10-Second Stress-Release Valve

This is a simple technique to quickly release stress and psychological tension. If you're feeling overwhelmed or overcome by emotion (fear, grief, anger, etc.), this technique can provide a channel for the instant release of that energy, leaving you calmer and more centered. This is an easy exercise with dramatic results.

1. Visualize a small sphere of white light on the front surface of your abdomen, about four inches above your belly button (in front of your stomach, about halfway between your belly button and the lower tip of your sternum).
2. Visualize the sphere moving to a point a few feet straight out in front of you, then focus on it for ten seconds or more. Notice any stress or tension streaming from your abdomen into the sphere, as if a plug has been removed, and then dissipating. The longer you focus on the sphere, the more you'll release.

You can try this with your eyes open or closed, and experiment with how far out in front of you to visualize the sphere.

Chapter 4-4
1-Minute Peace Meditation

Because inner peace already exists within you at all times, achieving inner peace is simply a matter of shifting your focus to that peace. When you're feeling stressed, or anytime you have a moment, use this technique to reconnect with your source of inner peace:

1. Say inwardly "I am peace," or simply "peace."
2. Visualize a peaceful white light filling you and overflowing into the area surrounding your body and out about eight feet around you. Take three deep breaths, visualizing the light becoming stronger with each breath, pausing after each to watch the light getting stronger.

The longer you hold your focus on this, the greater the shift into a more peaceful state. Try this with your eyes open or closed (but don't use it while driving or other activity that requires your attention).

Chapter 4-5

Prayer

When you involve yourself in prayer with the Divine, you're connecting into an all-powerful source of unconditional love, acceptance, and healing. Placing yourself into the presence of the Divine through prayer can create an immediate internal shift as your consciousness elevates toward soul and self-limiting dynamics are released. In prayer you can vent, express gratitude, explain how you feel, disclose your opinions, ask for advice, or whatever comes forward within you. Whatever you say in prayer, the effect on you is likely to be uplifting.

Remember to always ask for the highest good of all concerned when you pray (see also "The Highest Good of All Concerned," p. 18). When you do that, what comes forward as a result may be even more of what you want than what you originally thought you wanted. Because the Divine is perfect, its action is perfect. And because the Divine is perfect, its love is perfect and it provides perfectly, even if we don't know what we need to ask for.

When you pray, also remember that we don't actually know what's best for others, and we don't even know what's truly best for ourselves. Sometimes we're quick to judge an event as "bad" when it might actually be the perfect thing to lead you where you need to go next.

The same is true when we think about others. You may think you know what's best for someone else or what they should do or how they should be, but you don't have perfect information. You don't know what experience they need to have in order to learn a particular lesson, what steps may take them where they need to be next, or which path may end up bringing them joy and meaning. So when faced with imperfect or partial information (which is pretty much all the time), pray for the highest good of all concerned. Then you can be assured that whatever happens is for the highest good, even if you don't understand how or can't see how yet.

Part IV: Quick-Fix Toolkit

If you pray for a particular thing to happen (for the highest good of all concerned) and you get something different, maybe that thing wouldn't have worked out well for you, wasn't the best timing, or would have led you off-track or caused you to miss something important.

Without perfect knowledge and understanding (which none of us have), one of the safest and most powerful prayers we can make is to ask for Divine presence and Divine light for that person or situation for the highest good of all concerned. In fact, this prayer is so all-encompassing and complete that it could be the only prayer you ever need to make.

Chapter 4-6

Perspective

If you're dreading something or something particular is bothering or worrying you, putting it into perspective can instantly shift your viewpoint, reduce stress and mental pressure, and dissipate the emotional charge. Here are some examples of ways to shift your perspective about a particular matter:

- Ask yourself, "What if this experience has shown up right now for a reason? How can I learn from it or use it to my advantage?"
- Consider how you can use this experience as a stepping stone to what's next or to propel yourself toward an experience you want.
- Consider how you'll feel about this a year from now, five years from now, ten years from now, or when you get toward the end of your life. Chances are that it won't seem as big a deal anymore ("Oh, yeah, I remember that time when that thing happened"), and you might not even remember it.
- Consider your place in the universe. You are one person among billions on Earth. The Earth is just one of hundreds of billions of planets in the Milky Way galaxy. The Milky Way is just one of billions to trillions of galaxies in the universe.
- Acknowledge that it's not the end of the world. Life will go on, although it might be different.
- Focus on what's going well, even if it's just "the small stuff."
- Congratulate yourself on being here now and willing to step up and handle whatever is going on. Way to go, you!
- Don't compare yourself to others, and don't compare your process to others' processes. You are unique and so is your process. We each progress in different ways and at different speeds. It's not a contest. The point of personal growth is to keep moving onward and upward.

- Consider the adage, "If you don't like something, wait a while and it will change" or "The only thing that is constant is change" (ideas attributed to attributed to Mark Twain and Heraclitus, respectively).
- Remember that "This too shall pass."

See also the related techniques of Acceptance ("Chapter 3-2: Acceptance," p. 43) and Reframing ("Chapter 3-6: Reframing," p. 65).

Chapter 4-7
Identifying Your Next Step

Taking action can alleviate stress immediately. Even just identifying one step to take can be enough. When you're feeling overwhelmed or unclear, simply ask yourself, "What's my next step?" Depending on how stressed you're feeling, your next step could be something as simple as taking your next breath, or it could be to take responsibility for your own reaction (see "Owning Your Reactions," p. 48) or work through an issue to neutralize the trigger of your stress (see "Chapter 3-1: Working Through an Issue," p. 38).

When identifying your next step, you don't have to try to anticipate all the steps down the line. Narrowing your focus to your single next step enables you to set aside the stress of trying to figure out the following step, and the one after that, and exactly how you'll get to the end goal. You don't need to know all the steps to get from here to there. Just take the next step, and when that step is completed identify the one after that.

Consider an example in which you receive a notification from the utility company saying your electricity will be cut off in two weeks because you haven't paid your bills. Ask yourself, "What's my next step?" You might decide to check your bank account balance, look at the calendar to see when your next paycheck will arrive, or call the utility company and ask for a payment plan. At this point, you're not thinking about how you'll pay next month's or next year's bills. You're focused only on what your next step will be right now. Once you've taken it, you can ask yourself, "What next?"

Keep in mind that in any situation, one thing that's always a great first step is to call in the light, which can immediately reduce stress, enhance clarity, and focus your consciousness on the highest good for all involved (see "Calling in the Light," p. 17).

Chapter 4-8
Preparation and Contingency Planning

One way stress benefits us is by heightening our awareness during times when action is critical to our survival. Ages ago when all humans lived in the wilderness, stress was our "security mode" that kept us on high alert for possible animal attacks or other dangers. These days, stress keeps us on high alert to avoid different kinds of threats. But regardless of the nature of the stress triggering event, one way to reduce your level of stress is to prepare for the anticipated or feared situation by deciding how to handle or avoid it. When you've thought through the possible outcomes and are prepared to handle them, your stress is likely to decrease considerably because you know you're prepared.

The following steps can relieve stress through preparation and planning:

1. Thinking about the potential event or situation about which you're concerned, consider the possible outcomes and consequences if that did occur, focusing on the ones that are most likely and the worst-case scenarios.
2. For each possible outcome you feel you need to prepare for, make a plan for how you could avoid it, prepare for it, and handle it if it occurs. Also include contingency plans for how you'll handle unexpected or less likely outcomes, consequences, and ramifications of your (and others') actions.
3. Put your plan into action and make your preparations, as you feel is appropriate.

(To assist in decisions involved in your planning process, see also "Chapter 3-14: Decision Making," p. 95.)

Chapter 4-9
Releasing Undesired Dynamics

Sometimes negativity or darkness can show up within you and begin affecting you in a stressful way. Because you are "master of your domain" within your consciousness, you get to say what is and isn't allowed there. In any moment, you can release a stress-triggering dynamic from your consciousness by intending to release it and then allowing it to go. Some examples of dynamics that you might want to release include:

- Judgments ("Chapter 3-5: Forgiveness," p. 61).
- Negatively-charged labels ("Chapter 3-6: Reframing," p. 65).
- Limiting or inaccurate beliefs ("Chapter 3-7: Transforming Beliefs," p. 68).
- Negative self-talk ("Chapter 3-9: Transforming Negative Self-Talk," p. 75).
- Outdated decisions ("Chapter 3-11: Revisiting Past Decisions," p. 85).
- Agreements with yourself that no longer work for you ("Chapter 3-13: Renegotiating Outdated Agreements," p. 90).
- Limiting patterns.
- Others' opinions and expectations.
- Others' beliefs or judgments you've internalized ("Chapter 3-7: Transforming Beliefs," p. 68, and "Chapter 3-5: Forgiveness," p. 61).
- Emotional residues you picked up from others (anger, etc.).

When a stress-triggering dynamic shows up within your consciousness you can release it before it has a chance to take hold and start a stressful cascade within your consciousness. As you practice releasing these dynamics you'll likely start to notice instantly when a negative dynamic appears, which you can then immediately release. After more practice, you may notice that these dynamics don't enter your mind very often in the first place.

Always call in the light before you release anything from your consciousness, which can help ease the process and ensure that you don't get rid of something that you be better off keeping around (at least for now). It's also wise to ask that any negativity be transformed within the light (rather than it hanging around and affecting others, for example).

Releasing an undesired dynamic and its residual effects is a process, meaning it may not happen instantly. Often, the initial release of the dynamic only takes a minute, but the residual effects may continue to shift and release for some time longer. Healing and rebalancing can take place for up to an hour or sometimes even a few days. Also, after you release a stress-triggering dynamic, the physical effects of the stress itself may take up to an hour (or more) to subside as the stress biochemicals decrease and the body rebalances.

Sometimes when you try to release a dynamic, it may not leave. It may feel like it's not shifting or it's "stuck." This can indicate that there's another dynamic "locking it in." For example, before you can release a judgment with a lot of emotion attached, you'll need to express that emotion first in order to "unlock" the judgment so you can release it (see "Chapter 3-5: Forgiveness," p. 61). Likewise, if you're working through an issue that involves multiple underlying dynamics (such as judgments, self-limiting beliefs, and outdated decisions), you may not experience a shift with that issue until you've released all of those dynamics involved.

(Another type of dynamic you can learn to release is an imagined scenario, which you can read about in the next section, "Chapter 4-10: Releasing Imagined Scenarios," p. 178.)

How to Release Undesired Dynamics

To release an undesired dynamic, follow these steps:

1. Call in the light by inwardly saying, "I call in the light and ask for release and healing for the highest good of all concerned and I ask that any negativity be transformed within the light."
2. Inwardly say, "I release..." and then the dynamic you are releasing (for example, "I release my judgment of myself as not deserving respect"). Visualize it leaving you and flowing into the light.
3. As the dynamic leaves, you may feel an energy shift within you or you may sense a greater lightness or sense of peace within. If you don't feel a shift, consider other related dynamics that may need to

be released before the first one can go (such as expressing associated emotions or releasing an inaccurate belief).

Examples of releasing statements include:

- "I release the belief that I am not a capable person."
- "I release my decision never to accept help from others."
- "I release my judgment of my sister as wrong for worrying about me."
- "I release the label of 'disaster' I used to describe this situation."

How to Do a Broad Release

A broad release is a way to release many dynamics at once without needing to identify each one individually. For example, you can release all the negativity you picked up from other people that's affecting you right now without having to name each judgment or bit of anger you're sensing. Always include "for the highest good of all concerned" at the end to ensure that you release only the things serve you to release (for example, some negative dynamics may still have value because they will prompt future healing within you).

Examples of broad release statements include:

- "I release all negativity within me that no longer serves me, for the highest good of all concerned."
- "I release all residues, effects, results, reactions, repercussions, ramifications, etc. that no longer serve me, for the highest good of all concerned."
- "I release all imagined scenarios that do not serve me, for the highest good of all concerned" (for example, imagining how someone else feels when you don't really know, and your imagined version is creating stress within you).

A broad release may leave behind some things you need to release individually, so if you're still experiencing "not peace" within yourself, look for any remaining dynamics that need individual attention or are "locked in" (such as by unexpressed emotion, as discussed earlier in this chapter and in "Chapter 3-4: Processing Emotions," p. 58).

Chapter 4-10
Releasing Imagined Scenarios

Be careful not to stress yourself by creating imaginary scenarios in your own mind. If you've ever caught yourself imagining a scary, worst-case scenario, you've experienced the power of your imagination to trigger stress within you. When we don't have complete information about a situation (what is happening or will happen, who is involved, whether you're in danger, etc.) our imagination tends to fill in the information gaps with possible scenarios. This imaginative speculation can actually benefit us by helping us think things through and prepare for pending threats, and although these made-up stories may initially provide some value, they sometimes continue triggering stress needlessly. Other times they merely trigger stress without providing value at all. So when an imagined scenario shows up in your mind, consider whether it serves you. If not, you can release it and relieve the stress associated with it.

Sympathy-Based Scenarios

Consider an example in which you've heard a news report that someone far away is suffering from an illness. You notice that you've created a very detailed mental picture of what that person is going through, what their experience is like, what they're feeling and thinking, what's happening around them, what others around them are doing and feeling, etc. Then you react to that imagined scenario in a stressful way with worry, sympathy (joining in the person's suffering), fear, judgment, and possibly other dynamics. Once you're aware of this imagined scenario, it's time to take a step back and evaluate what's going on in your mind. Consider the following:

- **Accuracy**—Chances are that the imagined version isn't accurate. Unless you have a detailed account from the person involved that tells

you how they actually feel and what it's like, your imaginary version is not much different than a story made up in a book or movie.
- **Value**—Consider whether this imagined story provides any value to you or the person involved. If you're not going to take action to help the person, then there's not much point in "wallowing in the suffering" along with them. You may find value in the scenario, such as if it enables you to protect yourself or others or to help the person involved (such as directly by going there, or indirectly by sending financial or other help, etc.). However, once you've decided not to take action (beyond perhaps sending light or praying), the imagined story becomes merely a source of stress that you might be wise to release.

Pay attention to how you handle news that triggers sympathy within you, and make sure you're not stressing yourself with a made-up story that doesn't help anyone but that distresses you. Often, the only result of imagining someone's suffering is that you jump into suffering along with them, creating a private world of suffering within your own mind. Instead, consider loving the person who is suffering, feeling empathy for them, helping them as you choose and as they will accept, sending them light, or some other productive action. In other words, when you notice yourself imagining a sympathy-based scenario, consider releasing the scenario and moving into empathy or action instead. As you practice this new pattern over time, it will become easier to catch and stop yourself in the act of imagining, thus avoiding the resulting stress and perpetuation of internal scenarios that don't serve you or others in any real way.

Fear-Based Scenarios

Another way that your imagination can work against you is when your mind creates imagined fear-based scenarios about the future. Although fear serves us well by prompting us to prepare for future challenges and threats, fear that's allowed to take over and run rampant can be more debilitating than helpful. When you experience fear about what might happen, you'd be wise to supplement that fear with a mental process that evaluates any potential threat and how best to handle it (see also "Chapter 4-8: Preparation and Contingency Planning," p. 174). If the imagined scenario isn't helpful in any meaningful way, or once you've benefitted from any value, you can release it. If it won't release, consider whether there's another dynamic locking it in, such as strong emotion (see "Chapter 3-4: Processing Emotions," p. 58) or an irrational or outdated belief (see "Chapter 3-7: Transforming Beliefs," p. 68).

How to Release an Imagined Scenario

When you notice an imagined scenario in your mind:

1. Acknowledge that it is imaginary and you don't actually know the actual, full details (such as exactly what the person's experience is or what will happen in the future).
2. Evaluate the scenario. Consider whether it provides any value to you or anyone else, and decide whether you need or want to follow up (such as to get more complete information or take action to protect yourself or help others). Without any value or helpful action, all you're doing is making up a story in your head. If you decide to take action, then glean any value you can from the scenario to help you figure out specific actions (such as imagining what supplies might be most helpful in a disaster).
3. Release the scenario by saying inwardly, "I release this imagined scenario, and I send the light to all involved for the highest good of all concerned" (see "Sending the Light," p. 19).

Chapter 4-11
Observing Your Thoughts

The technique of observing your thoughts involves shifting into "inner observer" mode, simply watching what's going on in your mind rather than reacting to it. This technique is particularly helpful when you're experiencing stress or overwhelm, or as a mindfulness technique when you want to be aware of what's going on in your consciousness.

Observing your thoughts involves temporarily stepping back from your thoughts and into a higher, more neutral place from which your thoughts can't trigger negative reactions within you. In other words, you're choosing to center yourself in an inner place that's beyond judgment, opinion, worry, or other stressful reaction. Shifting into this mode provides several benefits:

- Moves you out of reaction mode and breaks the pattern of constantly reacting to one thought after another.
- Reduces the stress and other deleterious effects of reacting to your thoughts.
- Shifts your locus of control, empowering you to decide which thoughts to give energy to, "buy into," or perpetuate.
- Enhances inner peace because you're no longer engaging with whatever thought happens to shows up.

To shift into the mode of observing your thoughts, simply begin observing anything that comes into your mind. Whatever thought shows up, just observe it with the attitude of, "Oh, look at that thought that just showed up. Isn't that interesting?" Don't jump in and start evaluating the thought, labelling it as "good" or "silly," expanding on it, or anything else. Just watch and remain neutral. Eventually the thought will float away or be replaced with another one, which you will then observe.

Chapter 4-12
Setting Aside a Worry

If a worry is relentlessly gnawing at you, you can choose to set it aside and come back to it later. For example, if you wake up in the middle of the night worried about something, you can consciously decide to suspend the worry and reassess it tomorrow when you're fully awake and rested, when you can think through the situation, figure out how to be with it and how to handle it. (For more about planning and preparation as a stress-relief technique, see "Chapter 4-8: Preparation and Contingency Planning," p. 174).

Here are several specific ways to set aside a worry and to help reinforce that decision within your subconscious mind:

- Say inwardly, "I release this worry into the light and I intend for it to be resolved in the best way and perfect timing for the highest good of all concerned."
- Visualize the worry floating out of your consciousness up onto an imaginary shelf made of white light somewhere in the room.
- Write the worry on a piece of paper and set it aside, symbolizing the worry leaving your consciousness and flowing onto the paper where it will wait until later. You could even schedule an appointment with yourself on your calendar to revisit this worry at a certain time. This reassures your subconscious mind that you won't forget to deal with it.
- Do a free-form writing exercise focused on this worry, in which you pour onto paper all your thoughts and feelings about it, noting any solutions or insights for future reference (see "Chapter 3-22: Free-Form Writing," p. 127).
- Say a prayer asking for Divine assistance in this matter, releasing it into the guardianship of the Divine to be handled for the highest good of all concerned and with perfect clarity regarding your ideal involvement in handling it (if any).

Chapter 4-13
Focusing on a Keyword

When you're feeling stressed, scattered, or challenged in a certain area of your consciousness, a focusing keyword can help restore balance. Choose a keyword that focuses your consciousness and inner resources in a desired direction (such as "peace" or "creativity").

You can also extend this focus into a meditation by holding it longer (such as several minutes), allowing your consciousness to shift further in that direction, deepening your experience and drawing more deeply from the well of your inner resources. Sustaining your focus longer also creates a space into which your intuition, inner wisdom, and inspiration can speak, often bringing forward insight regarding the situation or issue that prompted this exercise.

You can choose any word or phrase as a keyword. Examples include:

- **A quality**—such as strength, courage, empathy, joy, kindness, or creativity. For example, if you're stressed you might inwardly focus on "peace," or if you're feeling vulnerable you might focus on "unconditional love" (which offers a form of inner protection).
- **A concept**—such as acceptance, trust, listening, forgiveness, nurturing, progress, opening your heart, or inspiration. For example, if you're finding it challenging to trust yourself you might focus on "trust," or if you're feeling downtrodden you might focus on "upliftment."
- **An aspect of your consciousness**—such as higher wisdom, loving heart, intuition, mind, or inner child. You can call on any aspect of your consciousness to assist you by focusing into that aspect. For example, for more clarity you can focus into your intuition, or if you need an expert on playing you can focus into your inner child. Feel free to get creative when calling upon your inner resources. For example, you can focus into your "inner artist" when selecting a new color palette for your house or your "inner inspector" when you need an eye for detail.

Chapter 4-14
Gratitude

Focusing on something for which you're profoundly grateful can instantly infuse you with peace and elevate your consciousness beyond any tensions of the lower levels. For best results, choose things for which you feel profound, heartfelt gratitude—things that resonate deeply for you. For example, you might say inwardly, "I'm grateful for Michelle being a source of light in my life," or "I'm thankful for the fresh chance that each new day brings."

Practicing gratitude can also have more profound, longer-lasting effects when you practice it as an ongoing process and mindset, by maintaining an "attitude of gratitude." You can reinforce this perspective of gratitude by keeping a gratitude journal which you fill with gratitude statements. You can also use the journal itself as a tool for upliftment by occasionally reading through it to refocus your consciousness and bring forward inner peace.

Chapter 4-15
Visualization

Visualization is a powerful technique to reduce stress, or to create almost any other desired effect within your consciousness. A visualization usually involves creating an imagined experience within your mind's eye that replaces your current reality (and any stress associated with it). Typically it takes the form of an inward process with eyes closed, lasting anywhere from a few seconds to 20 minutes or more. A visualization could involve simply imagining yourself in a particular environment, or it might include a series of actions or imagined events.

Regardless of format, each visualization has a particular purpose such as elevating your consciousness, bringing forward clarity, "trying out" a particular experience, or taking you into a deeper state of peace. Visualization usually creates some kind of beneficial shift in focus—such as toward peace, goodwill, or joy—and can also contribute to inner transformation and healing. Remember to always call in the light before you begin (see "Calling in the Light," p. 17).

You can choose a ready-made visualization or create your own, as described in the following two sections.

Ready-Made Visualizations

You can find a huge variety of visualization techniques online, in books, in apps, from music sources, and elsewhere. These visualizations tend to take the form of either an audio narrative that guides you through a process or simple written instructions to read and then follow once you've closed your eyes. Depending on the nature of the visualization, it may take you on a journey, focus on one or more personal qualities, or encourage transformation, healing, well-being, or something else.

One of the most powerful ready-made visualizations for dissipating the effects of stress and negativity is the Rainbow Visualization (see "Chapter 3-19: Rainbow Visualization," p. 118).

Creating Your Own Visualization

You can design your own visualizations in unlimited ways using your creativity and imagination. To come up with an effective visualization, consider the process or result you'd like and then use your intuition to tell you what would work well for you. Keep in mind the more vivid and inspired the imagery, the more likely it is to engage you (and your subconscious mind), and to always call in the light before beginning.

Here are some ideas for creating your own visualization:

- Create a simple visualization using the basic technique in "Chapter 4-13: Focusing on a Keyword" (p. 183), such as visualizing peace filling your being and extending out to others around you.
- Visualize a situation or location from the past to recreate a particular feeling or experience within yourself. For example, you might recreate a state of carefree relaxation by visualizing yourself relaxing on the beach from your Bahamas vacation, or you might recreate a sense of security and well-being by visualizing yourself next to the cozy fireplace in your childhood home.
- Visualize an "inner sanctum"—a safe, happy place within your consciousness to which you can retreat whenever you like. It could take on any appearance (such as a mountain cabin, mansion, little cottage, or your childhood bedroom) and you can decorate it any way you like. Be sure to call in the light to surround, fill, and protect it.

Chapter 4-16
Speaking to Love

If you're feeling upset, stressed, or burdened, an inner conversation with a loving source can be very uplifting and healing. Of course, you could talk with a loved one directly. But even if the conversation partner is imaginary, the unconditional love you experience is still real love with the power for inner transformation. For example, if you have a friend who is supportive and loving toward you in real life, even when you imagine talking with that person you feel love within yourself. Your heart opens and your consciousness lifts when you think of that person, which can enable healing within yourself. All unconditional love is healing if it's truly unconditional, whether it's coming from within you or from some other source. That love you feel can dissolve stress, heal, and transform (for more, see "Applying Love," p. 20).

You can imagine a conversation with a close friend, a relative, or someone you don't know but admire (living or not, or even a made-up person, since you can imagine anything you want). In this imaginary conversation you can vent, explain how you feel, express opinions, ask for advice, express gratitude, or whatever comes forward within you. As you interact with this imaginary "beloved one" you can:

- Work through issues, perhaps using techniques in this book.
- Release the emotional charge surrounding an issue by expressing your feelings.
- Talk through problems, which may lead to solutions or answers.
- Seek clarity about issues within you that need further attention.
- Open to possibilities for greater self-acceptance, healing, and inner peace.
- Confirm that you are loved and lovable, and confirm your love for yourself.

Chapter 4-17
Seeing Others as Souls

When dealing with a particular person, if you're finding it a challenge to connect with your inner source of unconditional love, practice seeing the person as the soul that they are. If you can't see them as a soul or recognize that pure light within them, then focus on trusting that reality. Everyone is a soul. Everyone in their deepest essence is a perfect soul full of love and light, even if that's currently obstructed by personality, ego, or other things (yours or theirs).

When you focus on seeing others as souls, you can instantly see through all their behavior, issues, patterns, and any other emotional and mental dynamics and see their soul essence shining through. Sometimes you might have the sense that you're seeing their inner child or a joyful self hidden within them. You'll know when you're seeing soul because you'll suddenly experience love and great joy within yourself as soul recognizes soul.

Sometimes it helps to imagine the person as they might have been as a child, which can make it easier to recognize the bright light of soul within them. Also remember that you don't know what that person is dealing with in their life or in their mind. You haven't walked in their shoes or lived within their consciousness. Maybe the person is doing their best with what they have and what they know. Sometimes it's enough to remember the person is a soul and to want the best for them, such as healing, learning, or whatever is needed for them to be a happier, better human being.

Chapter 4-18
Letting Go of Shoulds

Eliminating the words "I should" from your vocabulary can go a long way toward reducing stress. Anytime you think or speak the word "should," consider it a red flag that points to something within you that needs your attention. Underlying the word "should" usually lies a dynamic that isn't serving you well, providing an opportunity to transform an inner source of stress by reclaiming personal power and releasing judgments.

Think about it: when you say "I should," ask yourself, "Should, according to whom?" You're implying that someone other than you is in charge of you. When you allow yourself to think that you "should" or "shouldn't" do something or be something, you're giving away your power and responsibility for yourself. You're forfeiting your personal power to whomever is saying (or whomever you're imagining is saying) "should."

Consider an example in which you're thinking, "I should finish that report today." To see how you're giving your power away, finish the rest of that sentence: "I should finish that report today or my boss will be angry" (giving power to your fear of your boss's anger) or "I should finish that report today so people won't think I'm lazy" (giving your power over to others' opinions as you imagine them, and also judging yourself as lazy if you don't finish today). If you're thinking, "I should finish that report today because I made a commitment," that sounds better, but to fully take back your power and responsibility, make it an intention statement instead: "I intend to finish that report today" or "I intend to focus primarily on finishing that report today" or "I intend to spend two hours on that report today."

In another example, consider that the thought pops into your head that "I shouldn't chew my fingernails." Ask yourself, "Should, according to whom?" If the full version is "I shouldn't chew on my fingernails because Mom says so," you're giving power over to your internalized version of your mother. Now, if you were still a young child, your mother likely would know better than you, so you'd probably do well to listen. But as an adult, you are in charge of you. If you're thinking, "I shouldn't chew on my fingernails or people will think I'm insecure," you're giving power to the imagined opinions of others. If it's "I shouldn't chew on my fingernails because then they hurt and because I'm ingesting germs," then take charge and decide what you really intend: "I intend to allow my fingernails to grow be healthy" or "I intend that every time I want to chew my fingernails, I replace that with calling in the light" (or you might substitute another more innocuous behavior such as tapping your fingers on a surface).

Often when we think in terms of "should," what we really mean is that we intend to, want to, need to, or think it would be a good idea. In any case, you can take your power back and reclaim responsibility for yourself by using "I" language, such as statements starting with "I intend" or "I believe." If you end up deciding not do what you "should" do, or to do what you "shouldn't" do, at least decide that and then release any judgments of yourself. For example, if you're thinking, "I shouldn't eat that donut," finish that thought to completion, such as "I shouldn't eat that donut or I'll feel bad." Then make a conscious decision whether or not to eat it. Don't judge yourself for wanting to eat it, and don't judge yourself for eating it. If you decide to eat it, just eat it and enjoy it (unless it will cause an allergic reaction or otherwise harm you, of course). If you then think, "I shouldn't have eaten that donut because now I feel bad" then take back your power by transforming that statement into whatever you decide, such as, "I intend to find a healthier treat when I want a donut," or "I intend to bake my own donuts with healthier ingredients."

Now, you may think that there are some cases in which it may seem appropriate to give your power over to someone else, such as your boss or your relationship partner. Again, it's important to look at the full version of the "should" statement you're accepting in your head. If you're allowing your boss to tell you what to do, it's because you made a decision that you would work for that person when you took the job. You made an agreement that you would complete the responsibilities that she assigns and do what she asks you to do. Each time you do a task she assigns, you are *deciding* to continue fulfilling the previous commitment you made. But you are still in charge: you can refuse at any time. There may be consequences, but you *can* refuse. Ideally, if give your power over to someone else on purpose, you're doing it because you've *decided* to do so—which means you're still in charge of you.

Now think about when you think that someone else "should" or "shouldn't" do something or be a certain way. In this case, you are trying to

Chapter 4-18: Letting Go of Shoulds

make yourself the authority over them: unless this is your child or someone for whom you're directly responsible, you're trying to take responsibility for something that isn't your responsibility (which can be big source of stress, as discussed in "Chapter 3-3: Responsibility," p. 46). It's also an unhealthy dynamic to allow within your consciousness because you're judging that person. For example, if you think, "My neighbor Ian shouldn't just sit around all day," what you're actually saying is that you're judging him as wrong or bad for not doing more. That judgment darkens your consciousness and that of whomever you share your opinion, and it may deteriorate your relationship with Ian. You may not know the whole story. Maybe Ian is sick or tired or dealing with a challenging dynamic within his consciousness. Maybe he's busy doing things of which you're not aware, or maybe he just enjoys sitting around all day because he can. In any case, you're not in charge of Ian. You can ask him if he wants your opinion, or if his behavior is affecting you directly you can explain to him how it's affecting you. However, because Ian isn't your responsibility, it's not up to you to decide what he "should" or "shouldn't" do, and judging him as bad or wrong can only do harm. If anything, you could choose to react by setting an intention for yourself such as "I intend to balance activity and rest in my daily routine," or you could examine your underlying beliefs (see "Chapter 3-7: Transforming Beliefs," p. 68) or how you might be projecting onto Ian your own judgment of your desire to rest (see "Chapter 3-10: Exploring Projections," p. 78).

Chapter 4-19
Thinking Locally

When you're feeling stressed about a worrisome situation somewhere out in the world, "thinking locally" can be an incredibly effective technique for managing your emotional and mental reaction. For example, consider a situation in which you're experiencing extreme stress after hearing that in faraway part of the world there's been a scary event or there's a dangerous situation, desperate need, or someone fighting in support of a particular cause. Unless you need to take some immediate action to keep yourself or others safe, you can shift into the mode of thinking locally to temporarily reduce the stress burden within your consciousness. This isn't suggesting that you ignore or deny the situation, but instead temporarily focus your attention within your local environment as a means of maintaining your own mental and emotional well-being.

"Thinking locally" means focusing as locally as you need to in order to relieve stress within yourself. Start by acknowledging the immediate situation around and within yourself. Confirm to yourself that you aren't in any danger right now from the worrisome situation (unless you are, in which case taking action is a higher priority). More specifically, acknowledge that you're physically safe in this moment, that the room you're in is safe and secure, that your house or building is safe, that you have resources available if you need help (friends, neighbors, emergency services, hospitals, hotlines, etc.). Unless the situation is likely to affect you in your local area, you can let go of thoughts about the situation or the effects it's having elsewhere in the world.

If you're feeling extra stressed about the situation, you can focus *very* locally, meaning within your own consciousness. You are safe inside your own head where you can find a safe haven from the external stress trigger. Put your intentions and imagination to work creating a safe inner space for yourself that includes everything you need to feel secure, reassured,

Chapter 4-19: Thinking Locally

and comfortable (for example, ask for a Divine presence within you, shift into soul awareness, imagine your favorite things or places, colors you love, soothing music, people with whom you feel calm, etc.).

Here are the steps involved in thinking locally to reduce stress. The idea is to think as locally as you need to in order to relieve your stress.

1. Determine whether you need to any action for safety's sake, such as to protect yourself or others. If so, that takes first priority. If not, proceed to the following step.
2. Shift your focus to a limited area in which you feel safe. For example, if you live in Japan and you hear about an earthquake in Greenland, you might say inwardly, "I'm safe in my country." If you hear about a gas explosion several towns away, you might tell yourself, "My town is safe from that." If you're still experiencing stress, shift your focus even more locally. Here's a hierarchy of localities you could focus on:

Your country.
Your state or province.
Your county or district.
Your town.
Your neighborhood.
Your block.
Your house.
The room you're in.
The place where you're sitting or lying.
Your physical body.
Your inner world and imagination.

3. When you feel ready, you can revisit the broader situation and decide whether you need or want to take any action regarding it. If at any point you start to feel stressed again and need a break, return to Step 2. If the situation is ongoing, is not a threat to you personally, and requires no action of you, you can stay focused in that local area for days, weeks, or months, as needed. If you choose to, you could take action to help those involved, whether by sending the light or in some other way. (Be sure you're discerning between things that are your responsibility and things that are not, and being careful what burdens you choose to take on, as discussed in "Chapter 3-3: Responsibility," p. 46.)

Chapter 4-20
Reality Check

When we perceive something as a threat, that perception can trigger a stressful cascade of fears, resistance, defensiveness, imagined outcomes, worst-case scenarios, and other dynamics. This reaction can become a runaway train within you if you don't intervene. One way to temper a fear-based reaction and dissipate stress is to do a reality check, which involves demonstrating to your subconscious mind that your current reality is different from what it's imagining.

Because the subconscious mind often doesn't distinguish between real and imagined scenarios when choosing what to react fearfully to, if you want it to release a fear reaction you'll need to convince it that the fear isn't necessary because you are safe. You can do that by showing your subconscious mind an alternative reality (the actual one) through the window of your conscious mind as you use your eyes and ears to inspect your current reality—looking and listening around you, asking others around you, checking the news, etc.

Because the subconscious mind tends to understand images and concepts more than word-level information, showing it is usually much more effective than telling it. You may sometimes feel silly showing your subconscious mind things that your conscious mind considers obvious but that are necessary to disprove your subconscious imagined reality (such as looking in the closet to disprove an imagined monster lurking there).

Let's consider an example in which you've heard there's violence happening in a town 10 miles away. Your mind immediately jumps to an imagined scenario of that violence coming into your neighborhood and affecting you in your house. To head off your runaway imagination, you can "show your subconscious mind" the current reality by:

- Looking out your window to verify there's no violence on your street.
- Getting more facts from the news or your neighbors.

Chapter 4-20: Reality Check

- Checking on a map exactly where the violence is occurring and how far away it is.
- Reading what's being done about the violence, whether it's contained, the motivation behind it, and other information that can confirm that the violence is unlikely to infringe upon your safety.

Another example is watching a war movie that triggers within you a fear of being attacked. You might do the following reality check to reassure your subconscious mind that you're safe (even though your conscious mind already knows):

- Look around the room and verify that there are no threats.
- Check on others in the household and verify that they don't seem dangerous.
- Verify that all the doors and windows in your home are secured.
- Look out the windows and verify that there are no threats outside your home.
- Check the news and verify that there are no reports of danger in your area.

Another type of reality check involves disproving your imagined scenarios about what other people around you are thinking or feeling. In other words, if you're really worried about what's going on within someone else's consciousness, you can check with them directly by asking what's on their mind or asking for feedback. That person is then free to choose whether and how much to share. For example, if you imagine that a certain friend is judging you, you can ask them directly whether that's the case. Consider how much less stressful understanding the actual reality would be than continuing to imagine something really negative. You may discover that very often the person was thinking something completely different, such as "I was actually thinking what a great job you're doing" or "I was thinking how much I admire your strength." Whatever feedback they give, you're still the one who gets to choose what you do with it and how much power you allow it to have in your consciousness.

Chapter 4-21
Using Distraction

Distraction is a useful way to temporarily escape stress if you're in a situation where it's safe for you to "tune out" for a while. Engaging in an alternative activity that actively engages your mind shifts your focus from your stressful inner reaction to the new activity. The more involving the activity, the better, and it also helps if it's something you enjoy. For example, you might work on an interesting project or hobby, watch an exciting movie or interesting TV show, read a mystery, do a crossword, write or perform music, or solve math problems. Get busy doing something that's interesting or involving enough that time flies by without you noticing.

One of the most effective forms of distraction amidst stress is laughter. Good-natured humor shifts your focus out of your stress reaction into the lightness and joy of soul. Injecting humor into your inner dialog and interactions with others can immediately prompt you to release your stress reaction and disperse the effects it has created within you. Notice as you laugh how negativity drops away and you feel uplifted, and notice what a lasting effect that shift has within you.

Occasionally, distraction can be sufficient to recover from stress, but unless you've worked through the dynamics underlying your stress reaction (such as using the techniques in "Part III: Haven-Building Toolkit," p. 35), the stress may return when you encounter or remember the original trigger. So the sooner you address the underlying dynamics, the sooner you can experience inner peace regarding this trigger.

Chapter 4-22
Inspiration

Finding inspiration such as from quotes or books can lighten your stress load and provide comfort. Especially powerful are types of inspiration that help you reframe a situation, gain a new perspective on things, or see things in a way that's more useful or comforting. Some inspiration can even be powerful enough to lead to inner transformation and healing.

Look for inspiration that's uplifting, encouraging, insightful, and that deeply resonates with you. You can find many sources online, in social media, books, videos, groups (online and otherwise), or quote-of-the-day services that email or text you daily.

When you find a quote or passage that you experience as particularly powerful, use it as a consciousness-shifting tool by writing it somewhere you'll see it often. You may want to compile a collection of quotes that you find particularly inspirational, uplifting, or calming. You could even categorize them by the type of situation during which they've helped you, such as during stress, grief, anger, and so on.

Here are some great examples of inspirational quotes:

- "Life isn't about waiting for the storm to pass…it's about learning how to dance in the rain" —Anonymous
- "It is Love that holds everything together, and it is the everything also." —Rumi
- "Find a place inside where there's joy, and the joy will burn out the pain." —Joseph Campbell
- "Darkness cannot drive out darkness; only light can do that. Hate cannot drive out hate; only love can do that." —Dr. Martin Luther King, Jr.
- "A table, a chair, a bowl of fruit and a violin; what else does a man need to be happy?" —Albert Einstein

- "I have learned silence from the talkative, tolerance from the intolerant, and kindness from the unkind; yet strangely, I am ungrateful to these teachers." —Kahlil Gibran
- "Everything that irritates us about others can lead us to an understanding of ourselves." —Carl Jung
- "We ask ourselves, 'Who am I to be brilliant, gorgeous, talented, fabulous?' Actually, who are you not to be? You are a child of God. Your playing small does not serve the world." —Marianne Williamson
- "The best and most beautiful things in the world cannot be seen or even touched. They must be felt with the heart." —Helen Keller

Chapter 4-23
Focused Breathing

In moments of stress, focusing on your breathing can calm and center you. Attuning to breathing seems to connect us into the most basic essence of our "aliveness," prompting us to momentarily set aside any disturbances within.

Focused breathing is a simple technique with only one step: become aware of your breathing. You don't need to change your breathing pattern or anything else about your breath. Just observe as the air naturally moves in and out of your lungs, your chest or abdomen rising and falling, the sensation of cool air passing inward through your upper airway, body-warmed air passing outward, and so on. In this moment, you don't need to focus on or think about anything else. Just observe as your breathing continues, breath after breath.

Chapter 4-24
Heart Touchstones

A heart touchstone is an internal cue that instantly recreates within you a state of open-heartedness and unconditional love that you associate with that cue. You can use this as a tool to shift into the soul-based unconditional love within you. For example, notice how when you think about someone for whom you feel deep, unconditional love (like a parent, child, pet, etc.), you feel a shift within your energy as love begins to fill you. You might also notice that the love eclipses the tensions within your consciousness, which fade as you shift into a greater state of peace.

The most effective heart touchstones tend to be ones that you associate with a deep, profound sense of love—that "light up your heart" when you think of them. You can simply focus on that thought or memory whenever you'd like to shift into a more loving and peaceful state.

Chapter 4-25

Energy Work

Energy work is a practice that shifts the subtle energies of the body. Everyone has invisible energies throughout and surrounding their physical body, including its electromagnetic field. If you've ever sensed when a person was standing close by, you were likely attuning to their subtle energy field as it edged into yours. There are also subtle energies associated with the dynamics of the mental, emotional, and subconscious levels of your being. An imbalance or disturbance in the energy on any of those levels can indicate an area that needs attention, such as for healing, releasing, or transforming. Energy work can facilitate shifting the dynamics underlying the disturbance, sometimes even restoring balance without identifying what the disturbance was. Energy work can:

- Bring issues to the surface that are ready to be worked through or healed.
- Assist in clarifying and shifting the underlying dynamics of an issue.
- Prompt unexpressed emotion to start moving and flowing outward.
- Clear out negative energy resulting from interactions with others.
- Shift stagnant or "stuck" areas within your energy (old patterns, limiting beliefs, judgments, decisions, etc.).

Energy Work Modalities

There are many formal modalities of energy work, such as Reiki or The Electrical Matrix. Each modality may use its own terminology to describe the energy that fills, surrounds, and flows through the body, but they all involve working with that energy with the intention of improving well-being. Some modalities require more training than others. However, the modalities that require more training are not necessarily more effective. For example, you can become certified in Reiki I in as little as one day, or you can spend a few weeks to several months learning other specific modalities and more about the most effective ways to work with energies. More sophisticated approaches such as acupuncture usually require a multi-year program. If you decide to pursue training, look for a program that includes supervised practice to refine your technique and learn the important guidelines of energy work. To learn more about the various energy work modalities, explore the vast amount of information on the internet, in books, and from other related resources.

Working Only for the Highest Good

Regardless of the particular modality you choose, it's extremely important that you use it in a responsible, soul-centered way. This means your (or the practitioner's) acknowledging that you don't have perfect knowledge of what is needed, and instead invoking the wisdom of a higher power. In other words, what you think may be best for you and your body may not actually be, and if you blindly "fix" a problem the way you think it needs to be fixed, you may make it worse, deprive yourself of the real solution, or create more problems for yourself. For example, a pain in your leg may signal that something needs further attention or action there. However, trying to get rid of the pain through energy work may not serve you well because if the pain stops you might not address the root cause. Maybe reducing the pain would cause you to skip the visit to the emergency room where a doctor would have discovered and treated a life-threatening condition. We are not all-knowing beings, and we can't predict all outcomes and "ripple effects" of a particular action. Therefore, before doing any energy work, always call in the light and ask for everything to happen according to "the highest good of all concerned" (see "Calling in the Light," p. 17). It's also a good idea to ask for the healing and releasing of only whatever is for the highest good to heal or release.

Working from a Distance

Some energy work can be done across distances, even from the other side of the world, by sending energy in much the same way as when light goes when you send it (as described in "Sending the Light," p. 19). Although this may not make logical or intuitive sense, if you're working with a practitioner who's experienced with working from a distance, you can experience the results for yourself and come to your own conclusion.

Other Ways to Shift Energy

The invisible energies that are shifted during energy work can also be shifted in other ways. One specific way is to make the shifts directly within your consciousness using the core techniques in "Part III: Haven-Building Toolkit" (p. 35). For example, a disturbance in the energy of your mental level that's being created by a judgment can be shifted by consciously releasing the judgment (see "Chapter 3-5: Forgiveness," p. 61). A disturbance on the emotional level due to unexpressed emotion can be brought into balance by expressing that emotion (as in "Chapter 3-4: Processing Emotions," p. 58).

Spiritual exercises are very powerful for shifting imbalances and disturbances, during which spiritual energy can bring your energies back into balance (see "Chapter 3-18: Spiritual Exercises," p. 114).

Sometimes negativity or darkness can show up within your energy field that can be shifted through releasing or visualization techniques (see "Chapter 4-9: Releasing Undesired Dynamics," p. 175, and "Chapter 4-15: Visualization," p. 185). Specifically, the Rainbow Visualization is a fantastic example of a technique that can elevate the energy within and around you (see "Chapter 3-19: Rainbow Visualization," p. 118).

Chapter 4-26
Social Discernment

When you interact with another person, the energy from each person's consciousness is exchanged with the other. This is true whether words are spoken or not, because simply being in the presence of another person results in both people's energy affecting the other, even if the effect is very subtle. That's one reason it's so important to choose wisely the people with whom you surround yourself. This is called "social discernment."

A note about how "interaction" is defined here: "interacting" with others includes in-person as well as virtual interactions, such as on social media, texts, or email. It also includes one-way interactions—such as you "interacting" with someone delivering the news on TV, reading articles or books written by someone else, or watching someone on a (fictional or reality) TV show or in a movie. If communication is coming from another person, whether it's directed to you personally or to a large group, and whether you're observing in person or from afar, the energy that rides on the communication will affect you directly.

Stress is one form of energy that's "contagious" from one person to another, as is anger. Have you ever noticed that when you began a conversation with someone who was stressed, you suddenly began to feel stressed too? With practice, you can become more mindful of the effects of other people's energy on you, which are often so subtle you don't notice them (and then you wonder why you always feel angry or otherwise "off" after talking to certain friends).

Think about how you feel when you interact with each significant person in your life. Do you feel that you're seen, appreciated, and celebrated? Do you walk away feeling happier and more uplifted? You may notice that people who are more soul-centered are the ones who are more open, loving, honest, supportive, and have more "good vibes." Likewise, consider

Chapter 4-26: Social Discernment

the effects of your virtual one-way interactions, such as when reading a certain celebrity's social media posts or articles from a certain news source.

Every person is a soul, although the reality of that may be more obscured in some people than others. You may or may not experience awareness of that reality depending on the extent of lower-level factors (dynamics, patterns, issues, etc.) obscuring soul. You may find it more pleasant to interact with others who are more centered in soul (evident by their unconditional love and "bright light") and less restricted by lower-level issues because they're actively working on personal growth. You can also increase your ability to connect with others at a soul level by working to clear your inner obstructions to your own soul level (as discussed in "2. Remove Obstructions to Soul," p. 9).

You may want to consider limiting your interaction (or avoiding it completely, as is practical) with people who drain your energy, are generally unsupportive of you, or whose energy affects you in an undesirable way. Instead, consider investing in relationships that are mutually accepting and non-judgmental. Surround yourself with those who are filled with light and lightness—whose soul is evident through their goodwill and good humor. You might seek out groups who share similar soul-centered values (mutual support, kindness, championing each other, etc.), either in person or online through sites such as Facebook. You can also become more discerning about virtual and impersonal interactions in all forms of media (including social media) by choosing which energies and messages you allow into your consciousness.

Keep in mind that it doesn't serve you to judge someone with whom you don't like to spend time or whom you perceive as having negative energy. Most of us are dealing with things the best way we can with the skills and knowledge we currently have, and we're each making progress through life and our personal growth processes at our own pace. Whenever you notice you're labelling someone as "wrong" or "bad," release that judgment (as discussed in "Chapter 3-5: Forgiveness," p. 61).

Chapter 4-27
Environmental Discernment

The environments in which you choose to spend time can make a huge difference in your inner state, and using environmental discernment can help reduce your exposure to undesired conditions and effects. For example, avoiding locations with physical or other aspects you find stressful can avoid triggering stress within you.

One important tool for identifying a problematic environment is mindfulness, which means being aware of any physical, mental, or emotional changes within yourself while you're in that environment. When you're aware of how particular environments tend to affect you, you can choose to spend more time in those that work well for you (that reduce stress, encourage openness and creativity, etc.). You can also avoid particular situations that tend to result in stress, such as by limiting contact with triggers like certain individuals, news sources, websites, or social media channels. Of course, you can deal with any psychological stress triggers by changing how you react to them (see "Owning Your Reactions," p. 48, and "Managing Your Thoughts," p. 47).

Some of the environmental factors that can affect you in any particular environment include:

- The physical energies such as electromagnetic fields (of the earth, of power lines, etc.).
- Subtle energies (of people, physical materials, etc.).
- Radiation (natural and human-generated).
- Air quality (levels of oxygen and ozone, the presence of chemical toxins, pollution, allergens, etc.).
- Light energy (including color, source quality, natural vs. artificial, etc.).
- Sound energy (including noise pollution, mood-affecting music, distractions, etc.).

- Verbal and nonverbal communications and the energies that ride on them (such as in news, social media, etc.).

Next, let's take a closer look at the factors in both the physical and nonphysical categories.

Physical Factors

Each physical environment you experience imparts its own energy or "vibration." As an illustration of this, consider how different you feel on a beach than in an office cubicle. The Earth has its own magnetic fields and energies, and objects can also emanate their own energies (as everything is made up of atoms, each having its own energy). Although your experience of a location is partly due to your inner reaction to it and the mental labels you place on it (peaceful, unpleasant, etc.), you can also experience subtle effects from the energies emanating from the place itself.

Nonphysical Factors

Of course, a major nonphysical factor that contributes to your experience of that environment is the energy of any people there (see more in "Chapter 4-26: Social Discernment," p. 204). You may have experienced walking into a building and suddenly feeling that "this is a happy place" or "this place feels depressing." You may have been reacting to the energy of the place or the energy of the people currently there, or both. But there's another possibility. A building or house can also contain emotional residues left behind by people who have spent time there in the past, which is another reason you may get a certain sense about a particular place. You can think of energy residues as kind of like that orange film that's left behind after emptying a container of leftover spaghetti. Whenever a person experiences emotion, that flow of emotional energy often leaves residues around the physical space, such as along walls and in corners. This is one reason it's wise when you're working through issues to ask that any negativity be transformed within the light, rather than sticking around in the environment. Physical spaces can be cleared of these energy residues using energy work ("Chapter 4-25: Energy Work," p. 201), and sometimes are cleared out simply by new energy moving through the space.

Chapter 4-28
Physical Contact

Physical contact (such as hugging or sitting next to someone) provides great stress-reducing benefits such as a sense of well-being and an exchange of positive energy between the two people. When you're in physical contact with someone who's expressing unconditional love, that energy of love flows from their consciousness into yours. (By the way, you don't have to be in physical contact to experience that energy, since it can also flow in other ways such through eye contact and on the loving thoughts the person sends toward you.) A pet can also be a wonderful "loved one" to cuddle with, and they'll benefit from the closeness as much as you do. If your pet isn't so much into cuddling, you can connect in other positive ways through playing or other quality time together.

Be wary of contact with people whose energy could leave lingering negativity, such as people whose presence tends to result in your feeling stressed or angry. Pay attention to your intuition as to whether the person's energy feels negative or uplifting to you, or whether you feel comfortable or uncomfortable with that person. Always be safe and use your best judgment to protect yourself energetically and otherwise.

Chapter 4-29
Water

There's something almost magical in the power of water to calm, uplift, comfort, and "wash away" negativity. Some people also notice that water helps them feel centered, more spiritual, or more creative. You may also notice an immediate positive effect when you experience water directly, such as in a shower, warm bath, jacuzzi, swimming pool, or ocean. In fact, you may not even need to be in contact with the water for you to feel it's calming influence: consider how you feel when you're near a lake, ocean, or waterfall.

Also pay attention to the effect that the state of the water has on you. For example, moving water (shower, ocean waves, waterfall) may have a more dynamic influence on body and mind, while water that's still may be more calming. Snow and ice may have yet different effects. Pay attention to the particular transformations in your inner state when you're around different forms of water, and use them to your advantage.

Chapter 4-30
Music

In the face of stress, music is an easy and very potent tool for shifting into a more peaceful inner state. Consider finding music that soothes your subconscious mind, such as soft music with long continuous tones in major keys, which tend to feel more uplifting than minor keys. Keep in mind that your subconscious mind may have completely different tastes in music than your conscious mind. Music that you think of as hokey, sappy, or old-fashioned may feel pleasant, calming, or soothing to your subconscious mind. So try different styles of music, even if your conscious mind doesn't enjoy them. Give various songs a good try by playing each for a few minutes and then noticing how you feel. Pay attention to your body (is it relaxed and comfortable?), your mind (is it quiet rather than chattering?), your emotions (do they feel peaceful and calm?). Here are some categories of music to start with:

- Meditation music.
- Spa music.
- Relaxation music.
- Soft classical music.
- Soothing choral music.
- Nature sounds.

Two specific artists that create powerfully effective music to elevate the consciousness and bring forward peace are Liquid Mind (such as the song "In Fields of Peace") and Aeoliah (such as the song "Celestial Sanctity").

PART V

QUICK REFERENCE

To quickly determine which technique in this book might be helpful in a particular situation, ask yourself these questions. For each "yes" answer, refer to the indicated section of the book for more information.

In General: Am I experiencing stress but I'm not sure where to start?
- Go to "Calling in the Light" (p. 17) and "Chapter 4-2: Centering" (p. 165), then consider "Chapter 3-2: Acceptance" (p. 43), "Chapter 3-3: Responsibility," p. 46, "Chapter 4-7: Identifying Your Next Step" (p. 173), and "Chapter 3-1: Working Through an Issue" (p. 38). (If you're overwhelmed by stress in a way that feels dangerous or out of control, or that you can't handle on your own, seek assistance from a medical professional.)

Chapter 3-2: Acceptance (p. 43):
- Am I fighting against a particular reality, such as by saying "If only..."?
- Do I experience inner resistance when I try to move forward?
- Am I wishing a problem would go away rather than focusing on fixing it?

Chapter 3-3: Responsibility (p. 46):
- Is it mine, meaning is it my responsibility or do I want it to be?
- Am I trying to take on a responsibility that isn't mine?
- When upset, am I acknowledging my responsibility for my own reaction?
- Have I used the words "I should" in my inner dialogue?

Chapter 3-4: Processing Emotions (p. 58):
- Am I experiencing strong emotion?
- Are my feelings clouding my thinking?
- Is my anger getting in the way of seeing a problem clearly?

Chapter 3-5: Forgiveness (p. 61):
- Am I judging myself or someone else as "bad" or "wrong" in some way?
- Are my judgments of others keeping me from enjoying social interactions?
- Am I blaming myself or others or feeling guilty about the way I am?

Part V: Quick Reference

Chapter 3-6: Reframing (p. 65):
- Are my own opinions and biases clouding the way I view the world?
- Am I missing an opportunity because of how I'm perceiving a situation?
- Am I interpreting an event or interaction in a way that hurts or limits me?

Chapter 3-7: Transforming Beliefs (p. 68):
- Am I holding a belief that's hurtful or keeps me from loving myself?
- Am I limiting myself with an inaccurate "not enough," "not possible," or "can't" belief?
- Are there opportunities I'm passing up because of beliefs about myself or others?

Chapter 3-8: Setting Intentions (p. 71):
- Is there something about myself or my life I'd like to change?
- Am I disempowering myself with language such as "I'll try to..." or "I wish I could..."?
- Am I living in reaction mode, feeling like things "just happen to me"?

Chapter 3-9: Transforming Negative Self-Talk (p. 75):
- Does my inner dialogue bring me down rather than lift me up?
- Am I telling myself things like, "I can't do anything right" or "Bad things always happen to me"?
- Are the words I'm using in my head darkening my view of myself or the world?

Chapter 3-10: Exploring Projections (p. 78):
- Am I experiencing a strong judgment about a person or their behavior?
- Do I find myself blaming the other person in a relationship that I find challenging?
- Do I notice myself idealizing or idolizing another person and thinking I could never be like them?

Chapter 3-11: Revisiting Past Decisions" (p. 85):
- Am I limited by rules I made for myself years ago?
- Is my current pattern of thinking due to a decision that no longer serves me?
- Am I still trying to live up to outdated standards I set for myself?

Chapter 3-12: Completing Unfinished Business (p. 87):
- Is my to-do list filled with uncompleted projects and unrealized dreams?
- Have I left something unsaid or undone in a particular relationship?
- Does my energy feel sapped by incomplete tasks around my home or office?

Part V: Quick Reference

Chapter 3-13: Renegotiating Outdated Agreements" (p. 90):
- Do I feel overwhelmed by my commitments to others or myself?
- Am I experiencing unmet promises or expectations in my life?
- Have I made a commitment that I feel I can no longer fulfill?

Chapter 3-14: Decision Making (p. 95):
- Do I feel extremely stressed when I have to make a decision?
- Do I tend to make decisions emotionally rather than logically?
- When making a decision, do I often put it off until it's too late?

Chapter 3-15: Leaning Into Your Strengths (p. 99):
- Do I feel like I don't have much to offer others?
- Was there a hobby I enjoyed as a child that I'm not active with anymore?
- Am I judging a particular characteristic of myself that I could turn into a strength?

Chapter 3-16: Creating More of What You Want" p. 104):
- Do I find myself focusing on what I don't like about my life?
- When I get something I really want, do I tend to not be happy with it?
- Do I tend to think that buying things will make me happy?

Chapter 3-17: Deepening Your Spirituality" (p. 110):
- Do I feel unfulfilled but can't quite identify what's missing?
- Do I find myself repeatedly coming up against the same challenges?
- Am I feeling stuck or unclear about my life direction?

Chapter 3-18: Spiritual Exercises (p. 114):
- Do I wish to become more aware of the soul that I am?
- Am I experiencing stress, hurt, or other kinds of "not peace"?
- Do I feel unclear about myself, my life, or how I "fit in"?
- Am I affected by a "negative cloud" or self-defeating attitude?

Chapter 3-19: Rainbow Visualization (p. 118):
- Am I dealing with mental chatter, frenetic energy, or feeling scattered?
- Am I experiencing the after-effects of a stressful interaction or event?
- Do I feel unmotivated, uninspired, or unclear?

Chapter 3-20: Affirmations (p. 120):
- Does it seem like I'm not in charge of my own life or myself?
- Is there anything I'd like to change about the way I relate to myself?
- Am I repeating a pattern I'd like to replace with one that works better for me?

Chapter 3-21: Meditation (p. 124):
- Am I experiencing stress or overwhelm in my daily life?

Part V: Quick Reference

- Do I find myself losing focus or giving in to distractions?
- Do I tend to look outside myself for answers about my own life?

Chapter 3-22: Free-Form Writing (p. 127):
- Am I experiencing mental overwhelm or strong emotion?
- Do I feel unclear about a problem, decision, or something else?
- Am I trying to understand how I feel or what I think or about something?
- Do I want to feel clearer-headed in order to focus on a particular activity?
- Am I seeking insight or creative inspiration?

Chapter 3-23: Writing a Shred Letter (p. 132):
- Do I need to express my feelings in a way that's safe for myself and won't hurt others?
- Do I have something to say to a person that I can't in real life?
- Is there something I need to offload or unburden myself of?

Chapter 3-24: Mental Clean-Sweep (p. 135):
- Do I feel tired just thinking of all that needs to be done?
- Am I struggling to figure out where to start when tackling my to-do list?
- Have I promised to complete more tasks than I have time for?

Chapter 3-25: Sleep (p. 138):
- Are my days physically, mentally, or emotionally challenging?
- Is my sleep quality being harmed by my sleeping environment?
- Am I having trouble falling asleep due to worries or mental chatter?

Chapter 3-26: Dream Interpretation (p. 144):
- Does a certain dream seem important but I don't know what it means?
- Could I use greater insight into my own self-limiting patterns and dynamics?
- Is there room for improvement in the way I relate to myself and others?

Chapter 3-27: Dealing with Nightmares (p. 153):
- Am I experiencing nightmares but have no idea why?
- Do I sometimes wake up from a nightmare that then affects me for quite a while?
- Am I having trouble finding the value in my nightmares?

Part IV: Quick-Fix Toolkit Techniques (p. 161):
- Am I currently experiencing stress?
- Do I need to reduce stress immediately, but I don't have time right now to work through the underlying dynamics of my stress reaction?
- Would I benefit from a quick "vacation" from ongoing stress?

What Did You Think of This Book?

Tell the author what you liked about this book and what you would like to see more of in future books. Nancy Wagaman welcomes your comments, which you can share by posting them on the website of the book purveyor where you purchased this book, or by visiting NancyWagamanBooks.com and clicking **Contact** in the main menu.

Keep Exploring

Join the Author's Mailing List

To join Nancy Wagaman's mailing list, go to NancyWagamanBooks.com and click **Subscribe** in the main menu. You'll receive occasional updates from Nancy Wagaman, tips and news about her upcoming books and other personal-growth resources. Your email address will not be shared.

Social Media

Discover more information and inspiration by following Nancy Wagaman's social media accounts:

Twitter: @NancyWagaman
Facebook: facebook.com/IntuitiveConsultant
Linktree: linktr.ee/NancyWagaman

The Author's Websites

Learn more about personal growth, intuition, dreams, and inner transformation by exploring the free resources and updates on these sites:

NancyWagamanBooks.com

Nancy Wagaman's author website with information about her books and services, free resources, plus links to more help at the bottom of every page.

TheCuriousDreamer.com

A free online dream dictionary website with more than 15,000 dream symbols defined for personal growth by Nancy Wagaman. Try the convenient dream analyzer tool by typing a short description of your dream and then seeing a list of possible dream symbol meanings. Explore DIY dream resources, including meanings of common dreams, top dream symbol categories, and how to program your dreams using focused dreaming.

MyDreamVisions.com

Nancy Wagaman's professional dream services website dedicated to understanding dreams and their meanings. Get a professional dream interpretation from Nancy, and read how her interpretations are helping dreamers. Take advantage of dream interpretation tools, sample dream interpretations, tips for improving dream intuition and recall, and educational dream quizzes.

The Curious Dreamer Blog

An enlightening resource where Nancy Wagaman writes about dream interpretation, dream symbol meaning, and how to use your dreams to improve your life, as well as news about dream books, events, and more. To follow, visit NancyWagamanBooks.com/blog and click **Follow** in the header of the blog's main page.

Book Websites

Follow Nancy Wagaman on your favorite book websites to learn about new projects and resources, read reviews of her books, and receive announcements when she releases a new book:

Goodreads: goodreads.com/nancywagaman
Amazon: amazon.com/-/e/B07741C61H
Bookbub: bookbub.com/authors/nancy-wagaman

More Books by Nancy Wagaman

Take the mystery out of dream interpretation with The Curious Dreamer book series, which includes these books:

The Curious Dreamer's Practical Guide to Dream Interpretation

Your dreams are telling you what you need to hear every night. This book teaches you to understand them and unlock their transformative power.

Unlock the Power of Your Dreams

Like a personal dream coach, this book walks you step-by-step through interpreting your dream, finding the value in it, and using it to make positive changes in your life. You'll learn the four-part dream interpretation process, then choose from 40 powerful techniques to customize a robust interpretation experience. This book's tips, techniques, and examples demystify dream interpretation by drawing from various modern psychology disciplines and the author's years of client work.

Praise for the Guide

"You will become your own dream expert..."
—*Lesley Jones (Book Reviewer,* Readers' Favorite*)*

"A valuable source for dreamwork...This book is very practical and deals with the nuts and bolts on dreamwork, as well as how to take care of your tools."
—*Henry Reed, Ph.D. (Psychologist, "Father of the Dreamwork Movement")*

"Insightful...a great in-depth look into interpreting the content and symbolism of dreams...well-written, well-researched..."
—*Amy Shannon (Writer and Book Reviewer)*

"This book is a must for anyone interested in dreams..."
—*V. Nunez (Book Reviewer)*

More Books by Nancy Wagaman

"Takes the labor out of understanding dreams....made for curious people who want to understand their dreams through a quick and easy reference tool..."
—James Hart (Poet & Editor)

The Curious Dreamer's Dream Dictionary

This complete course in dream symbol interpretation puts the power of dream symbol meaning directly into your hands and opens the door to a new world of empowering dream knowledge.

1500 Dream Symbols to Improve Your Life

This dream dictionary teaches you to master the art of dream symbol translation and discover hidden pointers to your ideal life. You'll find specific steps, analysis techniques, tips for recognizing symbol meanings, and 1500 illuminating symbol descriptions that prompt you to explore both traditional and personal meanings (rather than the one-size-fits-all approach of most dream dictionaries).

Praise for the Dictionary

"This is the coolest book I've ever read about dreams!...Very easy to follow and understand."
—Melinda H. (Book Reviewer)

"Well written, well thought through, and definitely better than most of the competition on the market!...The author seems to have a real understanding of how dreams and the human mind work."
—Kim Anisi (Book Reviewer, Readers' Favorite)

"You'll start to understand how your subconscious mind works..."
—Jo-Ann Duff (Writer and Book Reviewer)

"A resource that triggers understanding and self-reflection."
—AvidBards.com (Book Reviewers)

"Well worth anyone's time. It will serve as my bedside resource for dream interpretation...You'd be surprised the information you could glean from this tutorial."
—Paul Falk (Author and Book Reviewer)

More Books by Nancy Wagaman

The Curious Dreamer's Dream Essentials

An introduction to dreams, brimming with practical tools and tips that open the door to the world of dream interpretation for personal growth.

All-in-One Dream Interpretation and Concise Dream Dictionary

Discover 11 keys to interpreting your own dreams in this introductory book from the author of *The Curious Dreamer's Dream Dictionary*. With these practical tips, translation tools, and analysis techniques, you'll be free to explore your dreams and unlock their transformative power. You'll discover symbolism shortcuts, intuition as a dream translator, step-by-step analysis tools, symbol meanings in a concise dream dictionary, dream answers, how-to's, and more.

Praise for the Essentials

"The perfect primer to start your journey…It's organized, concise, yet brimming with all of the basics you need…"
—Jacqueline Regler, MLA (Book Reviewer, The Johns Hopkins University)

"Easily the best book on the subject that I have ever read…guides you step by step…I will be definitely coming back to this book time and time again."
—C. Conn (Book Reviewer)

"Think of this book as a textbook on dream interpretation…Nancy Wagaman explains the relevant concepts, techniques and caveats as well as I've ever seen…She has a knack of explaining complex, vague concepts in clear words."
—Dr. Bob Rich (Psychologist & Author)

"A dream interpretation gem…don't miss this one!"
—Mel T. (Book Reviewer)

"This is the book to start with if you have any interest in learning to interpret your dreams.…She explains in a logical fashion."
—Edi McNinch (Book Reviewer)

Learn More or Buy

To read more about these books and read excerpts, visit Nancy Wagaman's author website: NancyWagamanBooks.com. To purchase the paperbacks, visit Amazon.com. The digital books are available through Amazon.com and most major online booksellers.

About the Author

Nancy Wagaman is a human technologies innovator specializing in personal growth and transformation. Her practical techniques enable people to transcend self-limitations and improve their lives. Rooted in science and intuition, Nancy's transformative techniques are practical and easy to use. Nancy began developing human technologies during her early career at Bell Laboratories, and she has also consulted and conducted research for corporate, university, and private clients. Her work has been featured in magazines, radio, and television. Nancy holds advanced degrees in applied psychology and communications, and bachelor's degrees in psychology and biology. She is the author of numerous books, the creator of *The Curious Dreamer's Dream Dictionary* website (TheCuriousDreamer.com), and has written extensively on applied psychology, intuition, and other personal growth topics.

Index

10-second stress release, 167
1-minute peace meditation, 168
acceptance, 43–45, 52, 62, 63, 101, 169, 187
    and projections, 78, 80
    as a stress reducer, 17, 31, 49
    by soul, 6
    in relationships, 205
    of your emotions, 59
affirmations, 25, 120–23
    pre-sleep, 142
    to create what you want, 107
agreements, 11, 90–94, 175
    and intention setting, 71
    and shoulds, 190
    in unfinished business, 87, 89
    responsibility for, 46, 50, 51
beliefs, 40, 42, 68–70, 110, 141
    others', 175
    releasing, 68–70, 175
    responsibility for others', 49
    self-defeating, 9, 24, 29, 32, 75, 80, 96
    self-supporting, 40
calling in the light. *See* light:calling in the
centering, 141, 165–66
centering statements, 9, 165–66
clean-sweep, mental, 135–37
contingency planning, 174
control, shifting your locus of, 17
creating what you want, 104–9
decision making, 95–98
decisions, past, 54, 85–86, 110
    outdated, 32, 41, 42
    releasing, 175
discernment
    environmental, 206–7
    of intuition, 30–31
    social, 204–5
distractions, 110
    as a stress reducer, 196
    as distracting yourself, 112
    centering for, 33
    reducing through meditation, 125
    reducing through spiritual exercises, 116
dream interpretation, 144–52
    benefits of, 148–49
    common symbolism, 146–48
    process, 149–52
dreams, toxic, 154–55
emotions, 7, 58–60
    and free-form writing, 127
    and irrational beliefs, 68
    diffusing through spiritual exercises, 115
    dissipating through meditation, 125
    locking in judgments, 64
    locking in other dynamics, 39, 59, 62, 68, 177, 179
    processing, 39–40
    releasing before sleep, 141
energy work, 201–3
environmental discernment, 206–7
fear, 33, 39, 59, 141, 149, 167, 179
    acceptance for reducing, 44
    and shoulds, 189
    and the soul, 6
    of imagined scenarios, 178, 179
    of working through an issue, 31
    planning for reducing, 174
    reality check to reduce, 194–95
    subconscious, in dreams, 153, 154–55
    unconditional love and, 22, 25
focus
    and perspective, 171
    as a stress reducer, 26, 167
    during distractions, 112
    enhancing through clean-sweep, 135
    enhancing through meditation, 125
    enhancing through spiritual exercises, 116
    in visualization, 185
    locally, 192–93
    on gratitude, 184

INDEX

on others as souls, 188
on your next step, 173
setting before sleep, 142
through affirmations, 120–21
through centering, 165–66
through intentions, 71, 73
to create what you want, 25, 32, 106
toward peace, 168
toward soul, 4, 7–9, 10–11
forgiveness, 61–64, *See also* judgments
free-form writing, 127–31, 141
    as a stress reducer, 182
    for clarity, 33
    for expressing emotions, 39, 42, 127
    for greater clarity, 30
    for greater peace, 127
    for overwhelm, 32
    to discover subconscious dynamics, 79
gratitude, 9, 113, 131, 132, 141, 184
haven-building toolkit, 35–160
highest good, 18, 140, 169, 177
    in energy work, 202
    in prayer, 140, 169
imagined scenarios, releasing, 178–80
inspiration, 197–98
intentions, 8, 10, 11, 17, 18, 20, 32, 71–74, 110, 143
    and responsibility, 46
    as agreements with yourself, 91
    for meditation, 125
    for positive self-talk, 76
    for spiritual exercises, 114–15
    for thinking locally, 192
    for working through issues, 28, 39
    power of, 22
    pre-sleep, 142
    to create what you want, 107
    to replace shoulds, 189
intuition
    during meditation, 125
    during spiritual exercises, 30, 116
    during stress, 30–31
    in creating visualizations, 186
    in decision making, 95–96
    in dream interpretation, 144–45
    of others' energies, 208
    to create affirmations, 122
issues
    acceptance and, 44
    and acceptance, 44
    and emotion, 59
    and intentions, 72
    and responsibility, 47, 53
    and unconditional love, 22
    desire pointing to, 105
    dreams resolving, 148, 156, 157
    energy work revealing, 201
    free-form writing revealing, 127
    other people's, 63, 205
    projection of, 80
    shred letters revealing, 132
    taking action on, 59
    working through, 9, 17, 25, 27–33, 38–42, 173, 176, 187, 207
judgments, 7, 9, 18, 24, 26, 29, 32, 38–39, 41–42, 43, 110, 141, 156, *See also* forgiveness
    and acceptance, 44
    and free-form writing, 127
    and meditation, 125
    and projections, 84
    and reframing, 65–66
    and spiritual exercises, 114, 116
    and unconditional love, 20, 22
    creating blind spots, 66
    in imagined scenarios, 178
    in unfinished business, 87
    locked in by emotions, 59, 62, 176
    of self, 75
    releasing, 61–64, 175–77, 205
keyword, focusing on a, 8, 20, 112, 113, 124, 186
light
    as a next step, 173
    as a stress reducer, 167
    calling in the, 17–19, 22, 25, 28, 164, 176, 185, 186
    for healing, 10, 165
    for peace, 168
    in centering statements, 156–57
    in energy work, 202
    in nightmare recovery, 156–57, 156–57
    in releasing process, 182
    in transforming negativity, 207

Index

of the soul, 3, 5
power of, 3, 197
sending the, 19, 179
to elevate the consciousness, 140
locally, thinking, 192–93
locus of control, shifting your, 17
love, unconditional
    applying, 20–23
    as a keyword, 183
    as a source of healing, 187
    creating more, 109
    from others, 208
    in self-talk, 75
    intentions for, 72
    power of, 20, 187
    soul as a source of, 5
    speaking to, 187
    the Divine as a source, 169
    to deepen into soul, 10
    touchstones for, 9, 200
    while working through issues, 39
meditation, 124–26
    1-minute peace technique, 168
mental clean-sweep technique, 135–37
mind
    as a stress management tool, 24–25
    as energy in motion, 24
mind mastery, 23–25
mindfulness, 22, 23, 24
    as a stress reducer, 25, 26
    in decision making, 97
    meditation, 124
    of agreements, 92
    of beliefs, 70
    of others' energy, 204
    of projections, 79
    of thoughts, 181
    of your environment, 206
    to reduce distractions, 112
music, 210
negative self-talk, 75–77, 110
next step, identifying your, 173
nightmares, 153–60
oath to self, 28
observing. *See* mindfulness
overwhelm, 16, 32, 53, 54, 88, 90, 118, 135, 146, 167, 173, 181
    free-form writing to reduce, 32

    mental clean-sweep to reduce, 135–37
peace, 3–4, 5, 7, 8, 9–10
    focusing on, 183
    from working through an issue, 38
    in dealing with nightmares, 158
    meditation, 1-minute, 168
    techniques to facilitate, 27
    through acceptance, 44
    through calling in the light, 17, 164
    through centering, 165
    through completing unfinished business, 88
    through decision making, 97
    through deepening your spirituality, 111
    through dream interpretation, 149
    through forgiveness, 63
    through free-form writing, 127
    through gratitude, 184
    through meditation, 126
    through music, 210
    through observing your thoughts, 181
    through processing emotions, 59
    through rainbow visualization, 118
    through releasing undesired dynamics, 176
    through responsibility, 53
    through sending the light, 19, 141
    through visualization, 185
    through working through an issue, 25
    through writing a shred letter, 133
perspective technique, 171–72
physical contact, 208
planning, contingency, 174
prayer, 39, 113, 140, 169–70, 182
preparation, 174
projections, 78–80, 78–84, 112
quick-fix toolkit, 161–210
rainbow visualization, 118–19
reality check, 100, 155, 160, 194–95
reframing, 65–67
releasing
    beliefs, 68–70
    imagined scenarios, 178–80
    judgments, 61–64
    outdated agreements, 90–94
    past decisions, 85–86
    stress-triggering dynamics, 175

Index

the effects of a nightmare, 155–56
through a shred letter, 132–34
through free-form writing, 127–31
undesired dynamics, 175–77
resistance to working through an issue, 31
responsibility, 46–57
  abandoned, in Toxic Dreams, 153
  and projections, 78–80
  as a stress reducer, 17, 51–52, 53
  as personal power, 46
  for agreements, 51
  for others, 49–50
  for self, 28, 47–49
  for your reactions, 32, 39, 48–49
  in relationships and interactions, 50–51
  intentions for, 72
  inventory technique, 54–55
  technique for taking, 53–54
  that isn't yours, 51, 191, 193
  to create what you want, 106
rules of stress management, 25–26
self-talk, 75–77, *See also* negative self-talk
shred letters, 132–34
sleep, 138–43
  calming yourself before, 142
  elevating your consciousness before, 140–41
  enhancing with meditation, 125
  enhancing with spiritual exercises, 116
  interrupted, 142–43
  releasing emotions before, 141
social discernment, 204–5
soul, 3–6
  as respite, 4
  centering in, 8–9
  committing to, 11
  deepening into, 10–11, 15, 29, 115
  experiencing, 5–6
  getting to, 7–11
  removing obstructions to, 7, 8, 9–10, 15, 205
  seeing in others, 188
  stress and the, 15–26
  tree model of, 4–5, 10
speaking to love, 187

spiritual exercises, 10, 30, 114–17, 140, 143, 203
spirituality, 10, 109, 110–13, 150
strengths, 99–103, 150
stress
  10-second release technique, 167
  and dream interpretation, 148
  and nightmares, 153–60
  and sleep, 143
  and the highest good, 18
  and working through issues, 25, 38–42
  comes from within, 15–17
  from outdated agreements, 90–94
  from past decisions, 85–86
  from unfinished business, 87–89
  indicated by projections, 80
  pointing to an issue, 25
  reducing through acceptance, 17, 25, 31, 49
  reducing through clean-sweep, 135
  reducing through decision making, 97
  reducing through forgiveness, 26, 63
  reducing through love, 25
  reducing through meditation, 125, 168
  reducing through mind mastery, 23–25
  reducing through mindfulness, 181
  reducing through preparation, 174
  reducing through processing emotions, 58
  reducing through reframing, 66
  reducing through releasing, 175–77, 178–80, 182
  reducing through responsibility, 17, 52
  reducing through self-talk, 76
  reducing through sleep, 138
  reducing through spiritual exercises, 115
  reducing through spirituality, 111
  reducing through transforming beliefs, 69
  reducing through visualization, 118, 185–86
  reducing with light, 18, 164, 187
  reducing with love, 20
  soul as respite from, 4
stress management, 24–26
techniques
  choosing, 31–33

INDEX

core, 29, 203
  getting started with, 31
  how to use, 27–33
thinking locally, 192–93
thoughts
  managing your, 47–48
  observing your, 181
toolkit, haven-building, 35–160
toolkit, quick-fix, 161–210
touchstones, 9, 40, 122, 200

toxic dreams, 154–55
trauma, 153, 155
tree model, 4–5
undesired dynamics, releasing, 175–77
unfinished business, completing, 87–89
visualization, 185–86
visualization, rainbow, 118–19
water, 209
worry, setting aside, 182